Routledge Library Editions

THE LIVING IMAGE

SHAKESPEARE

Routledge Library Editions – *Shakespeare*

CRITICAL STUDIES
In 36 Volumes

I	Shakespeare's Poetic Styles	*Baxter*
II	The Shakespeare Inset	*Berry*
III	Shakespeare	*Bradbrook*
IV	Shakespeare's Dramatic Structures	*Brennan*
V	Focus on Macbeth	*Brown*
VI	Shakespeare's Soliloquies	*Clemen*
VII	Shakespeare's Dramatic Art	*Clemen*
VIII	A Commentary on Shakespeare's Richard III	*Clemen*
IX	The Development of Shakespeare's Imagery	*Clemen*
X	Shakespeare	*Duthie*
XI	Shakespeare and the Confines of Art	*Edwards*
XII	Shakespeare the Dramatist	*Ellis-Fermor*
XIII	Shakespeare's Drama	*Ellis-Fermor*
XIV	The Language of Shakespeare's Plays	*Evans*
XV	Coleridge on Shakespeare	*Foakes*
XVI	Shakespeare	*Foakes*
XVII	Shakespeare's Poetics	*Fraser*
XVIII	Shakespeare	*Frye*
XIX	The Shakespeare Claimants	*Gibson*
XX	Iconoclastes	*Griffith*
XXI	That Shakespeherian Rag	*Hawkes*
XXII	The Living Image	*Henn*
XXIII	Shakespeare, Spenser, Donne	*Kermode*
XXIV	Themes and Variations in Shakespeare's Sonnets	*Leishman*
XXV	King Lear in Our Time	*Mack*
XXVI	Shakespeare as Collaborator	*Muir*
XXVII	Shakespeare's Sonnets	*Muir*
XXVIII	The Sources of Shakespeare's Plays	*Muir*
XXIX	The Voyage to Illyria	*Muir & O'Loughlin*
XXX	Shakespeare	*Nicoll*
XXXI	The Winter's Tale	*Pyle*
XXXII	The Problem Plays of Shakespeare	*Schanzer*
XXXIII	Swearing and Perjury in Shakespeare's Plays	*Shirley*
XXXIV	The Artistry of Shakespeare's Prose	*Vickers*
XXXV	Literature and Drama	*Wells*
XXXVI	Readings on the Character of Hamlet	*Williamson*

THE LIVING IMAGE

Shakespearean Essays

T R HENN

LONDON AND NEW YORK

First published in 1972
Reprinted in 2005 by
Routledge
2 Park Square, Milton Park, Abingdon, Oxon, OX14 4RN
711 Third Avenue, New York, NY 10017
Transferred to Digital Printing 2008
Routledge is an imprint of the Taylor & Francis Group
First issued in paperback 2013

© 1972 T R Henn

All rights reserved. No part of this book may be reprinted or reproduced or utilized in any form or by any electronic, mechanical, or other means, now known or hereafter invented, including photocopying and recording, or in any information storage or retrieval system, without permission in writing from the publishers.

The publishers have made every effort to contact authors/copyright holders of the works reprinted in *Routledge Library Editions – Shakespeare*. This has not been possible in every case, however, and we would welcome correspondence from those individuals/companies we have been unable to trace.

These reprints are taken from original copies of each book. In many cases the condition of these originals is not perfect. The publisher has gone to great lengths to ensure the quality of these reprints, but wishes to point out that certain characteristics of the original copies will, of necessity, be apparent in reprints thereof.

British Library Cataloguing in Publication Data
A CIP catalogue record for this book
is available from the British Library

The Living Image
ISBN 978-0-415-34901-7 (hbk)
ISBN 978-0-415-64783-0 (pbk)
ISBN 978-0-415-33086-2 (set)
Miniset: Critical Studies

Series: Routledge Library Editions – Shakespeare

SHOT-ON-HORSEBACK

'*The Angry Squire*'

The rider – like the fiery Douglas – is moving at a gallop, and brandishing (left-handed) a wheel-lock pistol, of which the cock can be seen.

The Living Image

SHAKESPEAREAN ESSAYS

T. R. HENN

METHUEN & CO LTD
LONDON

First published in 1972
by Methuen & Co Ltd,
11 New Fetter Lane, London EC4P 4EE
© *Copyright 1972 T. R. Henn*
Printed in Great Britain
by W & J Mackay Limited, Chatham

SBN 416 66220 X

Distributed in the U.S.A.
by HARPER & ROW PUBLISHERS, INC.
BARNES & NOBLE IMPORTS DIVISION

FOR H. S. BENNETT
*with admiration and gratitude
for many things*

by the same author:

LONGINUS AND ENGLISH CRITICISM
THE LONELY TOWER
THE APPLE AND THE SPECTROSCOPE
THE HARVEST OF TRAGEDY
POEMS AND PLAYS OF J. M. SYNGE *(ed.)*
PASSAGES FOR DIVINE READING
RUDYARD KIPLING
THE BIBLE AS LITERATURE
POEMS, 1964
etc.

Contents

ACKNOWLEDGEMENTS ix

Introduction 1
1. The Book of Sport 7
2. The Hawk and the Handsaw 21
3. The Ritual of the Hunt 41
4. 'The pleasant'st angling' 55
5. 'Incorps'd and demi-natur'd' 64
6. A Review of Bowmen 77
7. A Note on Shakespeare's Army 87
8. The Images of *Antony and Cleopatra* 117

SELECT BIBLIOGRAPHY 139

INDEX 143

Acknowledgements

I am, inevitably, indebted to many sources. Perhaps the chief, for the sections that concern Elizabethan field sports and horsemanship, there is a debt to D. H. Madden's *The Diary of Master William Silence*. For the ornithology I owe much to Edward Armstrong; both for his help and advice, and for his own works: in particular *The Folklore of Birds, Grey Wind*, above all for that seminal book, *Shakespeare's Imagination*. For the encouragement and interest that led to the Stratford Lectures – though their form and content have been much expanded – I am indebted to Professor T. J. B. Spencer, the Director of The Shakespeare Institute and Professor at the University of Birmingham. Part of the essay called 'A Note on Shakespeare's Army' was given at the Military Academy at West Point, with a demonstration of Elizabethan weapons and of some lessons that seemed relevant to those of the Second World War. I have included the essay on *Antony and Cleopatra* because the play seems to illustrate superbly the use of the imagery that I have discussed previously. But my debt is as great to the good fortune of a boyhood in the West of Ireland, where so much theoretical knowledge (both of wild life and of weaponry) had out of necessity to be proved by hand and eye.

For the primary works I have relied on those mentioned in the text; in particular *The Boke of St. Alban's*, Blome's *Hawking or Faulconry*, Gervase Markham, *The Master of Game*, Turberville, Ascham's *Toxophilus* and various books of the period on Elizabethan warfare. Among recent writings I am indebted in particular to three: Jorgenson's *Shakespeare's Military World*, Webb's *Elizabethan Military Science*, and Lindsey Boynton's *The Elizabethan Militia*. But perhaps my debts are greatest

ACKNOWLEDGEMENTS

here to my friend and former pupil, H. C. H. Mead, for an unpublished paper on *Shakespeare's Army*, written when he, a distinguished ex-Regular Officer, was reading for the English Tripos just after the War, and which he has most kindly allowed me to use. Another debt is to the Staff College course and its instructors at Camberley; and a third to the Curators of the Military Museum at West Point. To Martin Holmes (also an irregular soldier) I am indebted for allowing me to draw on his unrivalled knowledge of Shakespeare's London.

For the chapter on archery I have relied largely on Ascham (for that art has changed little) and particularly on a story called *Bowmen's Battle*, from Blackwood's Magazine of 1938, which I do not think has been republished.

I am also indebted to T. H. White's *The Goshawk* and *The Sword in the Stone*. It is over forty years since I drew his attention (when he was a pupil at Cambridge) to the hound and hawking language, and the art of fishing described in *England have my Bones*. But neither he nor I could have foreseen the present revival of falconry for strictly practical ends.

A final debt is to my present pupils. Among them is Trevor Park, who has given me much assistance. I have believed, and they have accepted, the need of a relationship where one of the most important things is that great poetry should come alive; and that if it cannot be proved upon the pulses in the course of teaching, it is at least possible to recreate the setting in our imaginations. And at the end I fall back, as so many critics have done for nearly two hundred years, on Dr. Johnson's Preface:

'He that will understand Shakespeare . . . must look for his meaning sometimes among the sports of the field, and sometimes among the manufactures of the shop.'

'War and Hunting, the two Fountains Of the River of Life . . .'

WILLIAM BLAKE

'Each creature is the signature of its action.'

KATHLEEN RAINE

Introduction

> Fish, flesh, or fowl, commend all summer long
> Whatever is begotten, born, and dies . . .
> W. B. YEATS,
> 'Sailing to Byzantium'

I

I think that this book began more than half a century ago, when I was a small boy at my home in the West of Ireland. I was much alone; and in the library I chanced upon a book of great delight, D. H. Madden's *The Diary of Master William Silence*. It had been given by the author to my grandfather, a fellow Irish judge. There was then much opportunity for reading, on wet days, and during holidays from my public school. My Mother and I, living alone together, were in a state of semi-siege, not unlike that of Spenser at Kilcolman Castle; I had the run of the demesne, 'the compass of a pale', and of the boats in the creek at the foot of the orchard. It became necessary, for purposes of food, to learn to trap and snare and net. For though I had shot with a full-bore gun since the age of eight – no firearms laws ran then in the West – and had been brought up in the strictest discipline of weapons, my father had died, most of the guns had been stolen by raiders, and, for the single favourite weapon that I had hidden in the rafters, there was no ammunition to be had. It is true that I unearthed a muzzle-loader of the 1840s, a Purdey built for my great-grandfather, and made shift to use that; improvising percussion caps with the heads of sulphur matches, and wads cut from cardboard. My experiences (not unsuccessful) with this gave me a lively appreciation of some of the difficulties that confronted arquebusiers of the Elizabethan Army. I made bow and arrows; but I did not then know Ascham's *Toxophilus*, which is still the Bible of any serious archer, and Irish yew, which is soft and fickle to work, did not render with arrows cut from a hazel grove. Nor was I yet aware of the symbolism that underlies both, or of that archetypal play, *The Philoctetes*.

II

The chief resources were the snare and the springe; sometimes the bow-springes operated by pleasantly complicated triggers that could be carved from wood, more usually the plain running-noose of twisted wire anchored by a cord to its peg. Half a century later I made and set them in a garden-border at Stratford, to show what the conspirators of *Twelfth Night* meant when they said of Malvolio that the woodcock was 'near the springe'. I have never been able to understand why the Elizabethans considered it a stupid bird. Those springes were of nylon, but some I made of twisted horse-hair to show the inwardness of Polonius' description of Hamlet's vows: 'Ay, springes to catch woodcocks'. When Wordsworth stole woodcocks from another's snares on the marshy places of the fells – the bird feeds at night in such spots, probing the soft ground with her long and exquisitely sensitive overshot bill – they too would have been of horse-hair; less visible than wire, and slightly elastic against the struggles of the bird.

A line of snares involved a round at dawn and dusk; lest the carrion birds, whom I hated with a kind of sensual violence, came to tear the rabbits. They gathered first, like the 'Corbies' in the Scottish ballad,[1] to 'pike out' the eyes. I went barefoot; partly to move more silently in the fields and woods, partly for the ecstasy, which I have not forgotten, of the touch of the grass, dew-covered, on the feet. It became clear, later, that Shakespeare was (perhaps uniquely) the poet of the dawn, and that one virtue of the Elizabethan hunt was to bring its followers to a hill-top as the dawn was breaking. In winter the snares became less effective: sometimes I borrowed ferrets, and learned to work and respect their exasperating qualities, and to tie that beautiful and complicated knot that muzzles them.

It was not until later that such experiences seemed to lift the curtain

[1] 'The Twa Corbies'.

INTRODUCTION

from one corner of the Shakespearean world. A paper now forgotten, 'Shakespeare's Field Sports' was,[1] I think, based largely on Madden. Some meditation on the work of other poets suggested that certain kinds of imagery were most effective when they were rooted in the concrete rather than in the abstract, and that this concreteness helped to explain (in some measure) the energy and the depth-content of certain kinds of images. Later came the knowledge of archetypal qualities, from Homer and the Bible. But there remained what one might call the problem of the psychology of the 'hunter' in certain situations.

In this a number of observations seemed to converge. The first was personal. Any 'hunting' activity includes, necessarily, periods of great concentration, often in a state of disciplined bodily stillness. I have vivid memories of waiting alone on a duck-marsh for the evening flight. In such conditions the senses are keyed up to receive and register a multitude of small impressions: the characteristic sound of a snipe dropping, invisible, through the dusk; a moorhen moving in the sedges; the faint crackle of tide-water rising among the stems of reeds. At the same time, another part of one's mind seems as it were isolated, released, because of the very concentration of the other part. The poet Roy Campbell once told me that he had known this on the high veldt, waiting on a hill for game. With Wordsworth it seems to have heightened his own sense of the numinous. A passage from Synge seems also relevant:

> The danger of his life on the sea gives him the alertness of the primitive hunter, and the long nights he spends fishing in his curagh *bring him some of the emotions that are thought peculiar to men who have lived with the arts*.[2]

Perhaps the conditions, the strength of the perceptions, lead on to an exactness of word. In the ballad of *Clerk Saunders* the ghost of Margaret's murdered lover appears at her window. He has to leave her at dawn – like Hamlet's father – to return to his grave or to Purgatory:

> O cocks are crowing on merry middle earth,
> I wot the wild-fowls are boding day . . .

[1] Afterwards published in *Essays of the Year*, 1934.
[2] *The Aran Islands*, p. 105. Italics mine.

Here the single word *boding* gives with great precision the low-voiced scattered talk of the birds, mallard or widgeon, while the light is still opaque.

III

I am not concerned in these essays with the problems of 'blood sports'. Beyond doubt our Elizabethan ancestors were more brutal, more hardened to pain and suffering of all kinds, than we are. The account of the public execution, and of its audience, in Nashe's *Unfortunate Traveller*, are damning enough. Bear and bull-baiting were (to us) revolting practices; as is cock-fighting, which still continues despite its illegality. One suspects that the 'drawing' of otters and badgers was equally cruel. So was the treatment of lunatics (consider Malvolio), and of idiots, of rogues and vagabonds. The 'shooting' of the time, with gun or bow, can, as always, result in wounding and great pain; the bow is more merciful than the gun.

But any naturalist knows that we must beware of projecting anthropomorphic feelings into the world of living creatures:

> Nor dread nor hope attend
> A dying animal;
> A man awaits his end
> Dreading and hoping all.[1]

The death of creatures in the natural state, surrounded as they are by every kind of enemy, is not more violent, or more pitiable, than those at the hands of the hunter or falconer. I think that as one grows older that oldest of instincts, the hunter's, tends to become less compelling; the preliminaries to a shoot, the training of dogs, the intimate experience of the countryside that such things give, is no less urgent, but the aesthetic revulsion from the destruction of grace and beauty by the shot-blast, intensifies. I have no regrets when I have killed for food.

These 'living images' from bird and beast, hawk, bear, wolf, dog, weazel, kite, crow, raven, chough – the 'poor hurt fowl that creep into sedges' – this fish flesh and fowl commend to us in every image their

[1] W. B. Yeats, 'Death'.

INTRODUCTION

intricate connection with 'the little world of man'. When Rubek the sculptor of Ibsen's *When we Dead Awaken*, turns bit by bit his masterpiece of man's nobility into the animal features that are his final revelation of humanity, we remember Lear, and the convergence of Man and Animal against that fierce background of the storm. Man, through the ages, has accepted certain animals as the symbols (which exist in their own right, and are therefore beyond explanation) of his religions and his fears. The psychologists have told us of their significance and endurance in many dreams; we know them in many guises in folk-lore, from the menace of the raven above the battlements of Dunsinane to the myth of the Wild Hunt and the skeins of geese (like a cry of hounds) on a moonlit night. It may well be that their presence in poetry is in part responsible for a strange excitement, of things perceived 'at the roots of the hair'. Or it may be that we are not yet so dulled by civilization that we cannot experience, through ancestral memories, something of their fresh concern.

And here a passage from *Richard Jefferies* (by Edward Thomas) seems important.

All this – the hunting, the reading, the brooding – was filling his brain, clearing and subtilizing his eye. The clearness of the physical is allied to the penetration of the spiritual vision. For both are nourished to their perfect flowering by the habit of concentration. To see a thing as clearly as he saw the sun-painted yellow-hammer in Stewart's Mash is part of the office of the imagination. Imagination is no more than the making of graven images, whether of things on the earth or in the mind. To make them, clear concentrated sight and patient mind are the most necessary things after love; and these two are the children of love.

And so this elaborate world of 'arte' and woodcraft, with its own highly technical terms, could not be mastered in action and in speech except through long study, or, preferably, by familiarity from boyhood. Shakespeare alone of all the Elizabethan and Jacobean dramatists uses it fluently, almost unselfconsciously, and often on occasions where its terminology might seem, at first sight, to have little or no connection with the dramatic current of his thought at the time. It provided him, almost continuously, with 'metaphors for poetry', as did those strange Instructors of Yeats's *A Vision*. Sometimes these metaphors are submerged, sometimes they do not yield up their contextual meaning unless we are prepared to learn something of this curious and now almost alien world of field-craft. But above all, there is apparent the great poetic power that integrates these images semantically and phonetically into the verse.

IV

It seemed likely that a poet or dramatist whose contact with natural objects has been made in this particular manner will use the relevant language with a freedom and unselfconscious energy that gives to his writing a special quality towards which I have tried to gesture in the pages that follow. One aspect of that is the *curiosa felicitas*, the essential rightness of the imagery; though it is essential to realize that this quality does not always emerge in its fullness unless the provenance of the imagery, and its complexity, are realized.

The object of these essays is therefore to re-examine some aspects of this technical language and some of the subtleties arising out of it. Hunting and war are closely linked in literature; and it therefore seemed fitting to discuss the language of war. In both my only claim is that of writing with some first-hand knowledge: of hunting, hawking, fishing, archery and horsemanship from my own experience in youth, and of war as a soldier. For though several books have been written on Shakespeare's Army there is only one that has been written by a soldier; and it is not common to have had practical experience with a variety of primitive firearms such as oppressed the Elizabethan soldier. In all this I have in mind the Platonic indictment in the Sixth Book of the *Republic*, and Milton's reassertion of it in the *Apology for Smectynuus*; and, in all humility, to claim some measure of dispensation.

But always the quotation from Coleridge is relevant:

> Shakespeare was no mere child of nature; no automaton of genius; no passive vehicle of inspiration possessed by the spirit, not possessing it; first studied patiently, understood minutely, till knowledge became habitual; and intuitively wedded itself to his natural feelings and at length gave rise to that stupendous power.

CHAPTER I

The Book of Sport

> O, like a book of sport thoul't read me o'er,
> But there's more in me than thou understand'st.
> *Troilus and Cressida* IV.5.238

I

The word 'sport' has several meanings in Shakespeare. Most often it suggests a trick, jest, or practical joke, some action leading to mirth. But here in Hector's rather improbable, even gratuitous reply to the menacing Achilles it has its own precise meaning. It is a Book of Sport that is in question. The Greeks, for all their subtleties, are barbarians; the Trojans are gentlemen. Achilles, says Hector, is as incapable of assessing character as he is of understanding the full implications of a 'book of sport'.

There were very many of them. The *Boke of St. Albans* by Dame Juliana Berners[1] was a kind of encyclopaedia: Isaac Walton borrowed much from it for his *Compleat Angler*. Gervase Markham's *The Pleasures of Princes* is equally generous in its scope. Turberville's *Book of Falconry* and Blome's *Hawking* are both technical manuals of the sport, and have much to say of the care of hawks in health and in their many ailments. Best of all, perhaps, is Gaston de Foix's *The Master of Game*. We must attempt to place these works in their general setting.

The 'sporting language' goes back to Norman times: some of its terminology persists today. It is aristocratic in its inception, ceremonious in its execution. Hunting in the great royal forests of the Norman kings, as in the smaller enclosure of the Tudor park, was a complex ritual. Both it and hawking demanded a number of servants and auxiliaries; keepers, foresters, huntsmen, grooms, kennelmen, warreners, falconers,

---

[1] There is no evidence that Juliana Berners, or Julyans Barnes or Bernes, was a Prioress of Sopwell Nunnery. See Gunnar Tilander, *Cynegetica*, XI.

'fishers'. Together they constituted a formidable body of retainers who were tough, skilled in fieldcraft and the use of weapons, and forming an important reserve for warfare. We may remember the importance of keepers, deer-stalkers and foresters in the formation of commando troops – such as the Lovat Scouts – in the Second War, and quote Gaston de Foix:

> For if he had need to go to war he would not know what war is, for he would not be accustomed to travail, and so another man would have to do that which he should.[1]

Their moral qualities, too, were fortified by hunting:

> And when hunters do their office on horseback or on foot they sweat often, then if they have any evil in them it must come away in the sweating . . . And since hunters eat little and sweat always, they should live long and in health. Men desire in this world to live long in health and in joy, and after death the health of the soul. And hunters have all these things.[2]

There were other aspects. The hunter, rising in the dawn, slept well and steadfastly all the night without evil thoughts of any sins. His life was a busy one, and so he must 'do his office without thinking of sins or of evil deeds'.[3]

In all this – the connection between Blake's 'two fountains' of war and hunting – we suggest an analogy with the tradition of the British Army (within living memory), of encouraging its officers in the exercises of pig-sticking and big game hunting, especially in mountain country, as inculcating the military virtues of toughness, courage, self-reliance, an eye for country, and speed of reaction in emergencies. And to the Elizabethan, as to the subaltern in India, his sport offered a welcome diversion from the ceaseless training in heavy weapons, and from the complex field exercises in horsemanship.

---

[1] *The Master of Game*, p. 13.
[2] *ibid*. p. 12.
[3] It will be remembered that the Renaissance philosophy of tragedy included the belief that all evil thoughts, as of murder and adultery, were generated at night.

THE BOOK OF SPORT

II

We should also remember the place of hunting in the Tudor economy. The Great House with its enclosed park was a miniature world. It was still largely feudal and self-supporting, ordered, like its gardens, with precision:

> Why should we in the compass of a pale
> Keep law and form and due proportion,
> Showing, as in a model, our firm estate...?[1]

The pale, the high fence or wall, designed more to keep the deer in than to keep poachers out, was to give its name to the defended strip, from Drogheda to Waterford, where the English power was consolidated after its various invasions of Ireland. On that same paling, as Surrey noted, stags would rub off their old antlers – 'The hart hath hung his old head on the pale.'

The herds that roamed the woodlands represented an important source of meat; their breeding was carefully watched, and the foresters' language to describe the various stages of growth and condition was precise. Juliana Berners gives a 'little herd' as 20, a middle herd as 40, a great herd as 60.[2] We know the complex technique, in part traditional in its ritual, of breaking up, skinning and jointing, the venison; and that knowledge was proper to a gentleman. We may note the pleasant superstition – not wholly dead – that the huntsmen should be given a drink of wine after the kill; otherwise the venison would putrefy. The thought came naturally to the conspirators in *Julius Caesar*:

> Let's kill him boldly, but not wrathfully:
> Let's carve him as a dish fit for the gods,
> Not hew him as a carcass fit for hounds...[3]

The provisions of *Leviticus* would seem less repugnant to modern man if he had to kill and dress his own meat.

[1] *Richard II*, III.4.40.
[2] *Boke of St Albans*, VI, 55.
[3] II.1.172.

THE LIVING IMAGE

There were the woodlands; the fish-ponds or stews (they too were liable to poaching) and the complicated devices for taking feathered game. Partridges could be netted, or kept (as in Chaucer) to fatten in mews. The dove-cote was an important source of food, and might – notably – be shaken by an earthquake.[1] Smaller birds might be netted: woodcock by hanging nets across their aerial paths in the woodlands through which they move in that brief period at dusk. Ratcliff, reporting to King Richard, uses the term with aptness:

> Thomas the Earl of Surrey, and himself,
> Much about cock-shoot time, from troop to troop,
> Went through the army, cheering up the soldiers.[2]

A common method of taking small birds when it was possible to ascertain their feeding places was by the springe, which may merit some description. Basically the springe or snare (the terms are interchangeable, in practice, though the springe is often taken to refer only to the bent-bow type) consisted of two parts: the running noose, and a cord attached to the noose and secured at a little distance by an anchor-peg. The noose itself was supported by a split twig of hazel, with the bark left on, so that the springe is supported at right angles to the feeding-ground, or, for hares and rabbits, between the beaten spaces of their run or meuse. For birds the noose was of twisted horsehair, or, for very small birds, of single strands. Three kinds lent themselves to capture by this means. The first group consisted of the woodcock and snipe which feed at night in relatively small areas: marshy ground near a spring, or, for woodcock in hard weather, under bushes, such as holly or laurel, which have thick varnished leaves and so keep the ground under them soft and moist. Such feeding places are tenanted year after year. A large number of horsehair nooses set among tussocks and marsh grasses would be moderately effective.

A third use of the horsehair springe was for catching larks, which were a prized Elizabethan delicacy. All small birds were additions to the

---

[1] *Romeo and Juliet.* 1.3.33.
[2] *Richard III.* v.3.69. (Q3, Q6 'cockshut'). The term survives: 'cock-shut light' is still used for winter twilight in Ireland. The text makes it clear that the troops are visited in the evening, *not* 'when cocks begin to crow'.

THE BOOK OF SPORT

larder, as on the continent today.[1] At the siege of Delhi during the Indian Mutiny, a doctor fired four barrels into a flock of sparrows, killing 150: a relief for the starving garrison. But the Elizabethans liked small birds in pasties. Shakespeare notes a certain contempt for this practice:

> We'll e'en to't like French falconers, fly at anything we see.[2]

Larks could also be taken by a device known as a *hingle*. This consisted of a long rope, to which was attached, at short intervals, hundreds of light horsehair nooses so that they stood out at right angles to it. This was then laid out in some field, preferably a newly-reaped stubble, frequented by larks, and close to a sunken ditch or cover. A small boy was stationed to throw his cap repeatedly into the air, himself remaining concealed. Larks, like golden plover, will come down out of curiosity to examine any strange object or event. Quite recently it was possible to see in French gunsmiths' shops the modern equivalent; a device rather like a metronome, driven by clockwork, so that a pyramid of mirrors revolved flashing in the sunlight. This attracts larks to where the sportsman is hidden with his gun. Essentially the same process is described in *Henry VIII*:

> If we live thus tamely
> To be thus jaded by a piece of scarlet
> Farewell nobility; let his Grace go forward
> And dare us with his cap like larks.[3]

There were other devices for taking small birds. One was bat-fowling, mentioned in *The Tempest*;[4] which was achieved by beating out bushes in which they roosted, or lighting fires near the spot to daze them; and then, as they flew out, catching them on nets suspended between poles.

The rabbit warren was an important source of food; and then as now the method was to interpose long loose nets hung on stakes between the

---

[1] Simenon notes the horror of an English detective, a guest of Maigret, when confronted with four robins as an entrée. In extenuation of the continental practice, we may point out that small birds and vineyards do not go well together.
[2] *Hamlet* II.2.430.
[3] *Henry VIII* III.2.280. The 'piece of scarlet' was the Cardinal.
[4] II.1.186.

THE LIVING IMAGE

burrows and the feeding grounds while the rabbits were out at night. Deer and hares were also taken in nets suspended in rides or runways through which the game was driven: such nets were known as *toils*, and are a frequent source of rather weak puns. The hare, to which a mass of folk-lore attaches and which has magical properties, is the object of bawdy references, as well as compassion for 'poor Wat'. Apart from coursing, the hare was taken in nets spread across her 'meuses' or runs The meat was strong, and valued (as today in the Fens) for its medicinal properties.

There was another method of taking small birds, whether for eating or for caging as song-birds. It was called *liming*. Implicit in the imagery arising from it there is a peculiarly nightmarish quality (like that of struggling in a mire or quicksand) which seems to have touched Shakespeare's imagination. He alludes to it thirteen times. Since liming has long been illegal, though I have seen birdlime for sale in Ireland as late as 1920, we may describe the process.

Birdlime is a white glutinous paste that dries very slowly. It was commonly made by boiling down the bark of the holly or willow. Its use was, perhaps is, a country pastime of small boys.[1] The lime was smeared on twigs where the birds perched or roosted, or on branches stuck into the ground, and the area below them baited with corn. But it was placed, not merely on a single twig, but on the neighbouring ones within the birds' wing-beat. On perching the feet became entangled. Then as the bird beat its wings in terror the feathers were caught again by other limed twigs. Claudius' soliloquy in *Hamlet* will serve as a norm; especially if we remember the archetypal imagery of the bird (and particularly the white bird),[2] as soul:

> O wretched state! O bosom black as night!
> O limed soul, that struggling to be free
> Art more engaged![3]

---

[1] Notorious then as now for their cruelty to birds, toads, cats and dogs. See Hogarth, *passim*. Wrens for the traditional processions of boys on St. Stephen's Day are still taken with birdlime: the dead wren is tied into a bush of furze. *v* Armstrong, *The Folklore of Birds*.
[2] *e.g.* swan, seagull, dove: as well as the idea of *upward* flight.
[3] III.3.68.

It is one variant of the *pitch-defilement-net-toil* group. For a modern parallel we may think of sea-birds caught on oil-polluted beaches.

Coursing, whether by single dogs or competitively by a pair on leash slipped simultaneously by the handler ('uncouple at the flying hare') was a favourite sport, particularly at the Cotswold Games, where Shallow's fallow greyhound was outrun. The hare-finder who accompanied the

. . . fawning greyhounds in the leash

had to have particularly sharp eyesight to spot the hare crouching in her form; hence the pun in *Much Ado* on Cupid (notoriously blind) as 'a good hare-finder'.[1] Today in frosty weather hares are often killed with sticks by noting the change in the colour of the grass, caused by the body-heat of the animal in the form where she is crouching.

III

The language, 'the termes of art' proper to all these activities, was technical and complex. The countryman, of whatever social rank, would know it and use it instinctively. To the *arriviste*, who had perhaps newly purchased an estate and wished to be received into circles which we should now call 'county', it presented a special problem. He had to learn this new language, as Mr. Jorrocks had to read up his hunting language and customs. The 'books of sport' were to hand: he might perhaps engage some young man to help him to assimilate them. It was a widespread and relatively harmless form of snobbery. A passage from Thomas Nashe's *Return from Parnassus* (1602) is relevant. The speaker is a former undergraduate, one Amoretto:

> When I was in Cambridge, and lay in a Trundle bed under my tutor [*i.e.* shared a chamber with him, sleeping in a truckle or 'camp' bed, as several undergraduates might do in an M.A.'s rooms, for their better morals] I was content in discreet humility, to give him some place at the table, and because I invited the hungry slave sometimes to my chamber, to the canvassing of a Turkey pie, or a piece of Venison, which my Lady Grandmother sent me,

[1] *Much Ado* I.1.182

hee thought himselfe therefore eternally possesst of my love, and came hither to take acquaintance of me, and thought his old familiarity did continue, and would beare him out in a matter of waight. I could not tell howe to rid myself of the troublesome Burre, than by getting him into the discourse of hunting, and then tormenting him awhile with our words of Arte, the poore Scorpion became speechlesse, and suddenly ravished. These Clearkes are simple fellows, simple fellows.

He reads Ovid [Perhaps it was the *Ars Amatoria*.]

This also throws some light on the relationship between an undergraduate and his tutor in the sixteenth century.

Beside it we may set a quotation from Ben Jonson:

Stephen. Uncle, afore I go in, can you tell me an we have e'er a book of the sciences of hawking and hunting? I would fain borrow it.
Knowell. Why, I hope you will not a hawking now, will you?
Stephen. No, wasse; but I'll practice against next year, uncle; I have bought me a hawk, and a hood, and bells,[1] and all; I lack nothing but a book to keep it by.
Knowell. O most ridiculous!
Stephen. Nay, look you now, you are angry, uncle: why you know, an a man have not skill in the hawking and hunting languages nowadays, I'll not give a rush for him. They are more studied than the Greek, or the Latin. He is for no gallants company without them.[2]

But the situation is not as remote as we might imagine. There are still many country houses today where it would be a *gaffe* of the first order to speak, say, of a flock of partridges or pheasants, of an otter's hole (instead of a holt). When P. G. Wodehouse writes of a small and objectionable boy that 'he ought to have been out at walk', not everyone will recognize the metaphor from walking hound puppies, to teach them behaviour and manners; before they are *entered* – again the technical word – with the rest of the pack. At our imaginary house-party we should not nowadays be constrained to speak with the

---

[1] It is interesting to note that a hawk's bell was used by Columbus' men as a measure for the three-monthly tribute of gold-dust imposed on each adult Indian.
[2] *Every Man in his Humour*, 1.1 (*cit.* Madden). (*Wasse* – I do not so intend.)

THE BOOK OF SPORT

meticulous accuracy that would have been expected in Shakespeare's time, and in which a page like Moth of *Love's Labour's Lost* would have been carefully drilled. No doubt a 'flock' will do for the starlings roosting in Whitehall instead of the conventional and expressive *murmuration*; nor should we often speak now of an *exaltation* of larks, though the word will recall much poetry. A *pride* of lions is still valid, as is a *bevy* of ladies, a *leash* of greyhounds. A shooting man will not often speak of a *stand* of plover, a *sord* of mallard, a *herd* of curlew, a *company* of widgeon, but he will be familiar with a *spring* of teal, a *gaggle* of geese (on the water), a *skein* of geese (on the wing), a *wisp* of snipe; not, nowadays, with the technically-correct *nye* of pheasants. Many of these nouns of collection are highly expressive of the behaviour and appearance of the animal. A wisp of snipe, for example, suggests the rapid scattering flight, the characteristic alarm-cry which is often rendered as *sceâp-sceâp*, and, in depth, the mysterious flittings of the bird to its feeding grounds at night. So, perhaps, in Roy Campbell's poem:

> The dead, like weary snipe, rising on high,
> Whined through the dusky pallor of the sky.

We have lost much of this language: such as *gladness* for a bright place in the wood, a forest glade; *tryst* for the stand where the hunter (like the Princess in *Love's Labour's Lost* when she hit the pricket) stood while the game was driven past, or moved of its own choice from *harbour* to pasturage. It was also important to speak appropriately of the 'crying' of the beasts. A hart *bellows*, a buck *groans*, a roebuck *bells*.[1] Even the operations of the gralloch were technical. A boar was to be *undone*: the tribe of deer were *flayed* after the head had been cut off; hares and rabbits were to be *skinned* without decapitation. Much of the language is of Norman origin. The familiar *Tally-Ho!* for example is a corruption of 'Il est hault – est il hault!' (the stag or boar is roused from his thicket or lair), which is gradually corrupted to "'til est ho – Tally Ho!' At the death of the seer the *mort* is blown on the horn. The huntsman cries out *Hoo arere!* – 'Back there!' as the hounds rush out of the kennel: *Swef, mon ami, swef* – 'Easy there!' when they are working too quickly. All the hunting cries to encourage the hounds seem to be from

[1] As does the sambur in India.

the French. The hawk *bates*, flutters her wings in fear or temper, which comes from the French *se battre*. *Forlange*, from the French *fort loin*, is the call blown when the stag has run out of bound or hearing, or the pack has out-distanced the mounted hunt: 'very far away'. A *berner* is a kennelman: from the French *bernier*, one who paid his feudal dues in the bran from which food was made for the Lord's hounds.

Let us take a concrete example of this technical language:

> Your tiercel's too long at hack, Sir. He's no eyass
> But a passage-hawk that footed ere we caught him,
> Dangerously free a' the air. 'Faith were he mine
> (As mine's the glove he binds to for his tirings)
> I'd fly him with a make-hawk. He's in yarak —
> Plumed to the very point. So manned, so weathered!
> Give him the firmament God made him for
> And what shall take the air of him?[1]

This is pastiche, a fragment of an 'Elizabethan' play. Its terminology is wholly accurate, but like all pastiches it betrays itself by its very richness. (We may think of Swinburne's imitations of Scottish Ballads where both vocabulary and alliteration is hopelessly overdone.) The Kipling passage might be paraphrased thus:

> This young nobleman has been loose without responsibility for too long. He's no tame home-bred chap, but a wild adventurous and experienced young man who'd done his first killing before ever he came here; and he's far too skilled and cunning. Indeed if *I* had control of him – as I'm the one that sees to his food – I'd see that he was put to some task with an experienced companion. He's just at the very peak of his powers, too: bursting with energy. He has been well-trained, and has learnt to deal with all situations. Give him the freedom and responsibility that is his due, and who shall get the better of him?

Embedded in the quotation are certain words which are familiar to Shakespeare readers. The *tiercel* is the male hawk, one-third smaller and lighter. The *passage-hawk* is one captured in free flight, from one point to another: *tirings* are the meat given to the hawk when it returns to the

---

[1] Rudyard Kipling, *Gow's Watch*, Act II.2 in *Collected Poems* (1960). A passage-hawk was sometimes called a 'passage'.

wrist. *Yarak* means in the prime of condition, eager to fly. None of these last three terms appear in the plays.

We may contrast this with the well-known passage where Othello speaks of Desdemona's possible unfaithfulness:

> If I do prove her haggard
> Though that her jesses were my dear heartstrings,
> I'ld whistle her off and let her down the wind
> To prey at fortune.[1]

The overt meaning of the passage is well known. Desdemona has been captured as a wild hawk (or 'passage hawk' as in the Kipling verses). She may or may not prove to be docile, faithful and obedient to her master. If she proves to be irreclaimable she must be abandoned as worthless. To fly a hawk down wind was tantamount to losing her. As a wild hawk she would then have to find her own living, presumably as a prostitute: as Cresseid in Henryson's story became 'commune' to the Grecian Camp. But there is some further imagery in depth.

In Elizabethan physiology the heart was seen as being attached to the lungs by a series of cords or threads. Sometimes these were imaged as the rigging of a ship: so

> The tackle of my heart is crack'd and burn'd,
> And all the shrouds wherewith my life should sail
> Are turn'd to one thread, one little hair.[2]

The jesses were the light leather thongs permanently fixed to the hawk's legs, and ending in light silver rings, the *varvels*, on which the owner's initials were stamped. These, like the small bells, were to assist in recovering a lost hawk. Through these rings was passed the *lease* or *leach* to be released by pulling through the varvels when the hawk was cast off. Among the submerged images are, perhaps, (1) the hawk is already, and permanently, carrying her jesses and varvels, which bear Othello's seal of ownership in the marriage contract;[3] (2) the jesses are, inexorably,

---

[1] III.3.264. Haggards could be difficult and inconstant: v *Twelfth Night* III.1.72, 'check at every feather'.
[2] *King John* V.7.52.
[3] Cf. *Canticles* 8:6: "Set me as a seal upon thine heart".

THE LIVING IMAGE

part of Othello's vital love for her; (3) if she is beyond reclamation he is content to lose her but at the price of losing part of his very being; the heart-strings would have been recognized by the audience as a symbol of life itself. 'When the heart expands' (this is one aspect of Lear's *hysterica passio*, the choking sensation of extreme anger) 'it cools and refreshes itself by means of air drawn from the lungs; when it contracts it expels smoky excrements by way of the lungs. "For the heart hath his filaments or small threads, apt and convenient for that purpose."'[1]

IV

The language of what would be called today 'shooting' is not of great interest and, save for one example, is not, I think, used with either spontaneity or depth. The reasons are not far to seek.

Guns suitable for fowling were not produced till the late seventeenth century, when the new techniques of making laminated barrels (as opposed to those bored from the solid, or even cast like a cannon) resulted in the development of weapons light enough to be used on flying or moving game. The last two decades of the eighteenth century saw the perfection of double-barrelled flint-lock sporting weapons at the hands of famous makers such as Egg, Nock, Manton. The flint-lock was superseded by the copper-cap, invented by the Scottish clergyman, Forsyth (*fl. c.* 1810). But it was the light fowling piece that, in conjunction with the Enclosure Acts, led to the emergence of the great estates, large-scale game preservation with all its attendant evils, and, indirectly, to profound changes in the sporting calendar of the aristocracy.

But in Shakespeare's time the only fowling piece was not unlike those recently used in the Fens of East Anglia. Such a weapon was immensely heavy, with a long barrel (as much as five feet or more)[2] and a short stock. Like the infantry musket it could not be fired except from

---

[1] R. L. Anderson, *Elizabethan Psychology and Shakespeare's Plays* (Univ. of Iowa Studies, III, No. 4).
[2] The long barrel was thought necessary to secure the complete combustion of the somewhat erratic powder.

a rest: either supported by a stalking-horse or from a camouflaged farm-cart, or poked over the edge of some bank or dyke to fire 'into the brown'. This inevitably resulted in a number of wounded or 'prick'd' birds, as with a modern punt-gun; hence Benedict's comment on the exit of the sulking Claudio:

> Alas! poor hurt fowl! Now will he creep into sedges.[1]

Shakespeare was what Chaucer calls 'pitous' towards animals; we remember Jacques' description of the wounded deer[2] and of Wat the hunted hare.[3] Perhaps the most vivid passage is that of the dispersion of the 'rude mechanicals' at the appearance of Puck:

> When they him spy,
> As wild geese that the creeping fowler eye,
> Or russet-pated choughs, many in sort,
> Rising and cawing at the gun's report,
> Sever themselves, and madly sweep the sky . . .[4]

As late as 1700 the 'creeping fowler' was advised to 'shoot slantwise' through the rising birds; and not to 'shoot at a single bird if you can compass more with your level'. It was not until 1727 that Francis Markland published his *Pteryphlegia*, or *The Art of Shooting Flying*, but this marked the beginning of the decline of falconry.[5] We may note Henry VIII's prohibitions against 'hand gunnes' (i.e. those capable of being used without a rest) and 'Haile shot'; the prohibition having an exemption clause for those who kept hawks. These were allowed to 'shoote Haile shot' in hand guns or Birding pieces at Crow, Chough, Pie, Ringdove, Jey or smaller birds for Hawkes meate only.[6] This was an early Statute of James I; Blome warns the falconer to be careful to remove the shot before feeding the hawks. Food is always a considerable

---

[1] *Much Ado* II.1.201.
[2] *A.Y.L.I.* II.1.33ff.
[3] *Venus and Adonis* 1.679.
[4] *M.N.D.* III.2.14. There has been much discussion among Shakespearean ornithologists as to the identity of the 'Choughs'.
[5] *v.* E. D. Cuming's Preface to Blome, *Hunting or Faulconry*, p. xxviii.
[6] *Ibid.* p. xxiii.

problem; we remember T. H. White in *The Goshawk*,[1] and his anxieties over providing pigeons and rabbits for his birds. That book, (and the film made from it in 1969) is the most readable of all adventure-stories in the manning of hawks. It ends in tragedy, as do so many histories of animals. In the next chapter we shall consider some of the details.

[1] It is also profitable to read certain chapters in various modern books of falconry.

CHAPTER 2

The Hawk and the Handsaw

The achieve, the mastery of the thing!
GERARD MANLEY HOPKINS, *The Windhover*

I

We must first try to put Elizabethan hawking into some sort of perspective. Shakespeare uses its terms of 'art' freely, spontaneously and with complete accuracy. No other Elizabethan or Jacobean dramatist does this.[1] Further – and this is important – he appears to use it not merely for his main dramatic imagery, but also for what is incidental: for 'the minute particulars' that fill up, as it were the margins of the pictures of character in action.

It involved the element of 'the chase', the pursuit of living creatures by others of their kind; but its efficiency as a means of obtaining food was negligible. A few mallard might be killed in the 'hawking at the brook', a few partridges in open country: later, after the introduction of the pheasant, one or two might be hunted, as in the naïve pseudo-ballad of anonymous origin:

> In the time of a summer's day
>   (The sun shone full merrily that tide)
> I took my hawk me for to play
>   My spaniels running by my side.
>
> A pheasant hen then gan I see,
>   My houndes put her soon to flight.
> I let my hawk unto her flee;
>   To me it was a dainty sight.

---

[1] I accept, without detailed verification in the *corpus* of Tudor and Jacobean Drama, Madden's assertion on this point.

THE LIVING IMAGE

But the true hawking was very different from this pot-hunting among the hedges: (and in summer too!) and from the 'sport' of knocking pheasants off their perches at night.

As an 'art' it was never, unlike hunting, a contribution to the economy of the great houses, though it claimed great antiquity; China, Babylon, Greece, Rome. In Shakespeare's time hawking had been known and practised in England for over five hundred years. In the reign of Henry II it was important among the recreations of the citizens of London. In Elizabeth's day the Royal Mews were situated in what is now Trafalgar Square.[1]

Above all it was hierarchical, ceremonious. The kinds of hawks that might be owned by various ranks, from the king downwards, were carefully prescribed. Punishment for the theft of a hawk was the same as for the theft of a horse. An instance is reported of a bishop excommunicating a parishioner who stole a hawk.[2] Hawks fetched high prices, and were royal gifts between princes. Hawking furnished matter for polite, ironic and parabolic conversation at the highest level; the opening scene of Act II of *2 Henry VI* is worth quoting in full. In the stage direction the entry of the characters is accompanied by 'Falconers hollaing':

Queen Margaret. Believe me, lords, for flying at the brook
I saw not better sport these seven years' day:
Yet, by your leave, the wind was very high,
And, ten to one, old Joan had not gone out.
King Henry. But what a point, my lord, your falcon made,
And what a pitch she flew above the rest!
To see how God in all his creatures works!
Yea, man and birds are fain of climbing high.
Suffolk. No marvel, an it like your majesty,
My Lord Protector's hawks do tower so well;
They know their master loves to be aloft,
And bears his thoughts above his falcon's pitch.
Gloucester. My lord, 'tis but a base ignoble mind
That mounts no higher than a bird can soar.

---

[1] Cuming, Pref. to Blome, *op. cit., passim.*
[2] *Ibid.* p. xxiv.

THE HAWK AND THE HANDSAW

Cardinal. I thought as much; he'd be above the clouds.
Gloucester. Ay, my Lord Cardinal, how think you by that?
Were it not good your Grace could fly to heaven?
King Henry. The treasury of everlasting joy.[1]

We may attempt some gloss on the passage. To fly a hawk in a high wind is as certain a way of losing her as releasing her down wind, as in Othello's image for Desdemona. Flying at the brook is dealt with below. Gloucester's falcon has been remarkable for the directness with which she flew towards the quarry, and the height she made above it preparatory to the stoop. An ascending bird of any kind may be an emblem of pride, ambition, strength; as the many eagles of the Bible. It is also, as in Jeremy Taylor's famous simile of the ascending lark, an emblem of prayer: which may be beaten back by anger, or the east wind.[2] It is used spontaneously of Caesar's supposed designs on the crown, and the tribune's denigration of him:

> These growing feathers pluck'd from Caesar's wing
> Will make him fly an ordinary pitch,
> Who else would soar above the view of men
> And keep us all in servile fearfulness.[3]

I know of no evidence that the wings of hawks were thus mutilated: rather the reverse, and I think that the image is compound and abstract. The main point lies in the implications of the last line; all birds cower, and are reluctant to fly, under the shadow of a hovering or passing hawk.[4] We may also note the moralizing piety of the King.

II

At this stage we may examine some of the qualities of the hawk as a living image. Its antiquity is considerable, from emblems of Horus onwards. Its qualities of strength, majesty, a certain inscrutability of gaze

---

[1] *2 Henry VI* II.I.I.
[2] 'Angry Prayer', *The Golden Grove*, No. 110.
[3] *Julius Caesar* I.I.75.
[4] I have known kites shaped like hawks flown over birds such as snipe or partridges to make them 'lie close'.

THE LIVING IMAGE

are added to those of wildness, and Hopkins' 'the achieve, the mastery' of the air. Both in the air and in repose it is one of the most graceful of all birds. Its traditional sense of mystery is challenged only by the eagle, the albatross, perhaps the heron. It is the only bird that can be tamed to achieve man's business without any link besides the trained will. That taming sets up a special bond; having at times, apparently, a male-female relationship. It is itself the product of endless patience, understanding, and in classical hawking, some cruelty. It kills with a slash of its talons, or by a sickle-cut from the beak. Aesthetically the spectacle of the pursuit, the dramatic struggle to gain height above the quarry, the exquisite stoop at immense speed, with half-closed wings, the lightning slash at the victim: all these were part of the appeal of falconry. For some of the depth-images connected with it we may refer to Ted Hughes' *Hawk in the Rain*, and the familiar passage from Yeats's 'The Second Coming':

> Turning and turning in the widening gyre
> The falcon cannot hear the falconer;
> Things fall apart; the centre cannot hold;
> Mere anarchy is loosed upon the world . . .

Here the falconer is perhaps man, or the human intelligence, that has lost control of what his intelligence has made; the gyre (a key-word to Yeats) being both the expanding spirits of a civilization that is nearing the point of disintegration as it widens, and the effort of the bird to sever its links with that which controls it. And connected with this archetype are a number of peripheral or ancillary images.

III

The process of taming, 'manning' the hawk was difficult and protracted, and appears to result in this love-relationship, not unmixed with exasperation and at times hatred. The process is well described in T. H. White's *The Goshawk* from which we may quote:

> No wonder the old austringers used to love their hawks. The effort which went into them, the worry which they occasioned, the two months of human

life devoted to them both waking and dreaming, these things made the hawk, for the man who trained it, a part of himself. . . . To the falconer, to the man who for two months had made that bird, almost like a mother nourishing her child inside her, for the sub-consciousness of the man and the bird became really linked by the mind's cord: to the man who had created out of a part of his life, what pleasure to fly, what terror of disaster, what triumph of success![1]

As with all wild creatures the bond is established by food, repeated handling, and familiarity with voice and gesture. With one exception the laborious process of manning is the same today as it was in Tudor England. Once caught, and fitted with jesses and varvels, the bird was temporarily blinded by sewing together the eyelids. This was the process known as *seeling*. It is used by Shakespeare four times to describe physical or moral blindness, sometimes reinforced by the idea of cruelty. The most famous and the most complex example is in *Macbeth*; moving (as so often) from the concrete to the abstract:

> Come, *seeling* night,
> *Scarf* up to the *tender eye* of pitiful day,
> And with thy bloody and invisible *hand*
> Cancel and tear to pieces that great bond
> Which keeps me pale![2]

Once blinded, the bird is starved, watched by day and night, denied sleep; until she finally surrenders, and begins to take food, and to submit to caresses from her master. This, except for the blinding, is the sequence of events in *The Taming of the Shrew*. It is the disastrous method attempted by Desdemona in pressing Cassio's suit on Othello:

> . . . my lord shall never rest;
> I'll watch him tame, and talk him out of patience;
> His bed shall seem a school, his board a shrift;
> I'll intermingle every thing he does
> With Cassio's suit.[3]

---

[1] White, *op. cit.* p. 37.
[2] III.2.46. I have italicized the words in the image-cluster: using Armstrong's term in *Shakespeare's Imagination* (q.v.).
[3] III.3.23. We remember the Importunate Widow of the Bible.

THE LIVING IMAGE

What follows is familiar and has often been described. The hawk is taught to sit on her master's wrist, and to take food (her 'tirings') there; to fly from perch to wrist; to fly short distances while attached to a *creance* (a lovely word), a length of fine cord; to come to the lure; to wear the hood, and bells to show her presence if she is lost. Finally, by stages, she is 'entered' on living things: small birds, a rabbit, some easy prey. Always she must be taken abroad with the falconer, among men and events, sitting on his left wrist, proud, curious, inscrutable. Always her health must be regulated by her diet. Much of the Elizabethan manuals is given over to the innumerable diseases of the birds, and their cure.

We may next try to suggest the difference between the contrived and the spontaneous uses of imagery. When Juliet invokes Night with

> Gallop apace, ye fiery-footed steeds,
> Towards Phoebus' lodging: such a waggoner
> As Phaethon would whip you to the west,
> And bring in cloudy night immediately.[1]

When Hamlet calls in his dramatically-assumed exuberance of grief (in competition with Laertes)

> . . . let them throw
> Millions of acres on us, till our ground,
> Singeing his pate against the burning zone,
> Make Ossa like a wart![2]

we recognize, however faintly ('notes are evils, but they are necessary evils'), the plundering of their store-houses of Latin grammar and phrase book, and of the infinite riches in the room of Ovid's *Metamorphoses*. When Donne says, in *Aire and Angels*,

> Whilst thus to ballast love, I thought,
> And so more steadily to have gone,
> With wares that would sink admiration,
> I saw, I had love's pinnace over-fraught . . .

I at least am not greatly moved, even when I find a contemporary

[1] III.2.1.
[2] V.1.287.

painting (by Bellini) of the Barque of Love, and Venus sitting in it with an enormous globe on her knees, and the little boat weighed down to her gunwales. But when Juliet says:

> Come, civil night,
> Thou sober-suited matron, all in black,
> And learn me how to lose a winning match,
> Play'd for a pair of stainless maidenhoods[1] . . .

I am, so far, mildy interested, and think about the image from tennis, perhaps of the submerged pun, if indeed there is one, on the *losing chace* of tennis, the *winning* stroke to the tambour. But when she goes on

> Hood my unmann'd blood, bating in my cheeks,
> With thy black mantle . . .

I am aware of a new excitement, an infinitely more complicated and subtle experience set moving by the image. For in some strange way the mysterious imagery that is related to the hawk seems, with its multiplex references, to be proper to tragedy. Juliet is as yet *unmann'd*, waiting for the bridal night: and here there is the triple pun. For she is as yet a maiden, she is frightened (*unmanned* in the other sense): the hot blood comes and goes in her cheeks, like great waves, in obedience to the throbbing pulse of fear, desire and excitement; *bating* being the technical word for the *unmanned* – unbroken – hawk fluttering wildly on the wrist or the weathering-block, to which it is secured by the jesses. She is untamed, *unmanned*: that wild beating will not be stilled till she is *hooded* by the darkness of the night, as the hawk is quieted into utter stillness by the hood slipped over her head. For the great hawks, fierce and powerful, are chosen from the females, a third larger than the male: so Juliet talks of her Romeo as the tassel (tiercel)-gentle, and would call him back with the lure:

> Hist! Romeo, hist! O! for a falconer's voice
> To lure this tassel-gentle back again.[2]

[1] III.2.10.
[2] II.2.158. Dover Wilson and Duthie note that a 'Tercil-gentill' is found in *The Boke of St Albans*.

THE LIVING IMAGE

So Hamlet, in hysteria, calls the wandering ghost whirling an imaginary lure round his head:

> Hillo, ho, ho, boy! Come, bird, come.[1]

III

The problem of obtaining hawks was a formidable one and the loss – always a possible accident – correspondingly great. They might be taken as fledglings from the nest, when they were known as *eyasses*, the term slightingly applied to the Boy Actors, the Children of the Chapel Royal, in *Hamlet*.[2] But the eyas was an uncertain quantity, difficult to rear, and held in some contempt. Almost as unreliable were the hawks taken near the nest when they were just able to flutter from branch to branch: they were then known as 'branches'. But the best hawks were fully fledged, had learnt to kill (had 'footed') in the wild state, and, in their first year, were known as 'soar' hawks.

The process of catching them was highly complicated; and since it has some bearing on a passage in *Macbeth*, we may attempt to describe it.

All birds are apt to mob intruders of whatever kind, especially strange ones. I have shot magpies and carrion crows with the help of a stuffed Victorian cat. Both of these may be 'buzzed' (in aircraft terms) by quantities of smaller birds. The owl, whenever it appears in daylight, appears to excite particular dislike.

> 'You must know that all *Birds*, that sleep in the *Night*, are enemies to those that take their Rest in the *Day* . . . You may with the smaller sort of *Owls* catch good store of ordinary *Birds*, as *Sparrow-hawks, Magpies, Jayes, Dawes, Blackbirds, Thrushes, Sparrows, Lennets* and the like: and with your great *Horn-Coot*, the *Goshawk, Faulcon, Lanner* etc. besides the aforesaid *Birds*.'[3]

The Horn-Coot or Eagle-Owl had first to be captured, tamed, and taught to fly between two perches. The process of training it took two months. Next, on a suitable site, a single tree, standing at least four

---

[1] Falconers used a soft whistle, or a sound made by 'chirping the lips together'; but not, apparently, the voice.
[2] II.2.342.
[3] Blome, *op. cit.* p. 1ff.

hundred yards away from any other, was stripped of its lower branches, and the ground in front of it cleared of brushwood. From the upper branches nets were hung from pegs in a V-shape. Spaces in the branches and above were to be filled with boughs:

> You must carefully gather up all the *Leaves, Chopings* and *broken Sticks*, and put them out of sight for the avoiding cuspicion; for *Hawks* especially are very jealous and observant.

Nets were then hung on the arms of the V, on pegs which could be pulled out with cords, so that the nets would fall forwards and downwards.

The Horn-Coot was then attached by a leash to the end of a long pole or plank, with some freedom to move between two perches on it. The plank passed over a pivot, so that it could be moved by the operator concealed among bushes. When this was done the owl fluttered enticingly. It was quick to perceive the presence of a hawk; inviting perches were left on the side of the trimmed tree.

> The *Bird* that was passing by having once discovered him, will presently stoop at him, and perceiving the *Tree* will take a *Stand*, to consider his strange Countenance and resolving to set on him.

At this stage the nets fall on the bird.[1]

The point is that the contemptible (and sinister) 'mousing owl' would have been familiar as the normal bait for this trap. That it should be mobbed and attacked by hawks was in the nature of things. That the owl should attack the falcon was the supreme and dramatic reversal of 'kind', wholly in keeping with the supernatural happenings on the night of Duncan's murder. Night and day became indistinguishable. Hence

> A falcon, towering in her pride of place
> Was by a mousing owl hawk'd at and kill'd.[2]

---

[1] We may compare this with the modern device of using a rocket to carry a net over a flock of birds so that they may be ringed and released.

[2] *Macbeth* II.4.14. 'Her pride of place' is not I think the highest point of her upward flight, but the height at which she prefers to 'wait on' above her master till the game is put up. There is a similar 'reversal of kind' in *Antony*

THE LIVING IMAGE

Other methods described by Blome include a kind of clap-net as used for plover, the bait being again the owl: capturing the 'branches' by means of ladders and short hand-nets: taking them with bird-lime: and by hand at night while they are roosting, with the help of ladders and a dark lantern.

The hawks procured by T. H. White came from Germany. He writes of a village in Holland (Valkensweard, Falconsheath) where the villagers made their living out of catching hawks in nets on their migration routes, and of the great prices paid at the auctions there by buyers from all over Europe.[1]

Once captured, whether eyas, 'branch' or haggard, the process of 'manning' went on with infinite patience. If all went well the hawk would learn, in progressively longer flights, to obey her master's whistle, to stoop to the lure whirled round the head, to return to the gloved left wrist on which she was carried. As a final achievement she would learn to 'wait on', that is to hover nearly motionless above the head of her master as he moved over the ground to put up the game, 'towering in her pride of place'.[2] She would learn to comport herself with calm dignity in any kind of company, without 'bating' or fluttering in nervousness or temper.

IV

From the falconer's point of view the hawks were divided into two classes, each with their own qualities and employment. There were the short-winged hawks, goshawk and sparrow-hawk, mainly used at

---

and *Cleopatra* (III.11.193) over the dove and the estridge, the short-winged hawk:

> Now he'll outstare the lightning. To be furious
> Is to be fighted out of fear, and in that mood
> The dove will peck the estridge.

It has been justly remarked that a dove pecking an ostrich – so several commentators – would not have been familiar in Shakespeare's ornithology.

[1] T. H. White, *op. cit.* pp. 143-4.
[2] We still speak of a 'towered' bird in shooting: when shot in the lungs it will rise perpendicularly to a great height, and thence fall dead. It always lies on the ground with the breast uppermost.

ground or low-flying game, particularly in wooded areas. They were flown from the fist when the game was sighted. The long-winged hawks, ger-falcon, falcon, lanner, hobby, kestrel, were used in open country, and were trained to 'wait on' above the falconer.

For either species – there are very many woodcuts and engravings – we must imagine a cavalcade or horseback, the falconer and spectators, the 'cadger' with a kind of frame suspended on his shoulders. On this the spare hawks were carried, hooded, on their perches.

For 'flying at the brook' as in the passage from *2 Henry VI*, II.I.I (this is the only allusion to it in Shakespeare) a stream was chosen with sedge or bushes along the banks and, preferably, with open ground for the horses on either side. Duck, and perhaps other minor wildfowl, were roused out of the cover with the help of spaniels and beaters with poles. If all went well the goshawk or sparrow-hawk would be cast off and make her kill. But the quarry might return again to the safety of the cover, or plunge[1] into the stream. It was then said to be *enewed*. The Folio spells it *enmew*, which some editions still read. The crucial passage is in *Measure for Measure*:

> This outward-sainted deputy,
> Whose settled visage and deliberate word
> *Nips youth i' the head*, and follies doth *enew*
> As falcon doth the fowl, is yet a devil . . .[2]

Onions gives 'drive (a fowl) into the water': Winny, 'drive into hiding'. Neither gives, I think, full force of the image. Part of it is clear: the new-revised laws against fornication strike at youth, as the falcon strikes at the neck with those deadly sickle-shaped talons: with the submerged meanings, perhaps, of youth *growing, pushing out*, like a shoot of a plant[3] – Shakespeare has used that idea before – and perhaps the stroke of

[1] Blome uses the expressive *plung*. I have seen mallard take to water in just this way.
[2] III.I.89. I follow Winny and others in this reading, instead of the frequent *enmew*. The former is much more in keeping. V. *The Boke of St. Albans* 'Your hawk hath enewed the fowl into the river'. The Folio reading is perhaps the result of a confusion between *enew* and *enmew*, to 'coop up'.
[3] Berowne is like an envious sneaping frost
That bites the first-born infants of the spring.
Love's Labour's Lost I.I.100.

the headsman's axe. But there is more to it than that. If the hawk missed, the quarry would take to water, or to a thicket. If the hawk attempted to follow into this last, she ran the risk of damaging a feather; later, perhaps, to be *imped* (*v.* p. 36). The malefactors of *Measure for Measure* merely 'go to ground': to water, or to the brakes. The security (and the shelter from the weather) of a brake of thorn or osier is comforting: hence the lovely image

> And when a tale is beautifully stayed
> We feel the safety of a hawthorn glade.

There *is* complete safety: and privacy. That is why I would keep the 'brakes of vice' in the same play:

> Some run from brakes of vice, and answer none.[1]

V

Herne or heron hawking offered, perhaps, the most spectacular examples of the contrast between hawk and quarry. For the herne did not go to ground or to thicket; it flew high, and pursuer and pursued strained to make height above each other, precisely like fighter aircraft. Like them, it attempted to 'make height' into the sun, so that the keenest eyesight was needed to follow the two birds, and to see which was gaining the upper station. But the whole passage is mysterious:

> I am but mad north-north-west: when the wind is southerly I know a hawk from a handsaw.[2]

However we read it there are difficulties. If we take 'handsaw' to be a corruption of 'hernshaw', Madden's explanation (following Clarke and Aldis Wright) is that on a bright morning with a strong north-north-westerly wind the bird would have been exceptionally difficult to pick out, but less so on the day of southerly wind and perhaps low cloud. Amstrong[3] makes out a strong case for 'handsaw' on the grounds of textual authority, and the quotation from J. Roy[4] 'He does not know a

[1] II.1.38. F1 – brakes of *ice*. I accept Steevens' emendation, as defended by Winny (*T.L.S.* 18 April 1958).
[2] *Hamlet* II.2.383.
[3] *Shakespeare's Imagination.* Revised Edition 1963, pp. 38–40.
[4] *Proverbs* (1768), p. 196: *cit.* Armstrong.

THE HAWK AND THE HANDSAW

hawk from a handsaw', as well as through the image-cluster relating to 'handsaw'. (Falstaff's sword 'hacked like a handsaw' – rapiers – goose quills). He goes so far as to admit the possibility of a pun: "It is likely enough that one so prone to equivocation as Shakespeare may have had in mind the pun 'handsaw-hernshaw', but it is certain that he wrote down plain 'handsaw'."

But my attention has been recently drawn by W. A. Wallace to yet another explanation, which is new to me. He tells me that to a builder in the West of Ireland a 'hawk' is the commonest of tools: a rectangular wooden platform with a handle beneath which is used for carrying mortar or plaster. A workman will say of a particularly stupid labourer 'He doesn't know a hawk from a handsaw' – *i.e.* he can't distinguish between two of the commonest tools. (It is not difficult to recall grosser modern equivalents.) It is quite likely that a usage of this kind should survive from Tudor times, or even from eighteenth century builders in Co. Mayo: countryfolk of those parts still speak, like Bottom, of a 'bottle of hay'.[1] But both this explanation, and Armstrong's seem to me to leave the matter of the two winds far from clear.

The heron, presumably worthless for food, is a shy creature. It would be roused, at some distance, from its fishing in the stream; 'at siege' is the expressive term. As a fisher it remains motionless for long periods, waiting for fish or eels to come within striking distance. According to folklore it carries some special scent on its legs or body to attract fish. It has magical qualities, because of its shape: there is a Celtic folk-tale of a man who stalks and shoots at a company of herons, and, going to retrieve his game, finds a dead hunchback. It occurs, fishing, frequently and in strange places in pictorial art.[2] In poetry it has anthropomorphic aspects; Dylan Thomas' 'heron-priested shore' is an echo of

> Nor can he hide in holy black
> The heron's hunch upon his back.[3]

---

[1] *M.N.D.* IV.I.35.
[2] *e.g.* in Bellini's *St Francis in Ecstasy*, in a mosaic in the dome of the Archbishop's Palace of Ravenna, in Chinese paintings.
[3] W. B. Yeats: 'Crazy Jane and the Bishop'.

THE LIVING IMAGE

Wounded, the heron will stab with its rapier beak, aiming for the enemy's eyes. An eighteenth century engraving shows a heron, which has just been brought down by a hawk, disgorging a number of small trout which a Scottish ghillie is collecting.

VI

On the weathering-block in the mews in the early morning, the hawks, taken from their perches, sat to preen themselves. There was a pan of water in front of each bird: she stepped in and splashed herself with water. Back on the block she 'bated', flapped her wings vigorously to flex the flying muscles. Next she would (like many birds) run each feather through her bill, which she had first dipped in oil from a gland near the tail, so as to cause the miraculous interlocking barbules to lie tight and close, presenting the most perfect aerofoil surface. For aquatic fowl the same process serves also to produce buoyancy in the water.

Sir Richard Vernon has been sent by the rebels to reconnoitre the Royal army before the Battle of Shrewsbury. He returns to the commanders to report. He has seen the enemy troops on parade:

> All furnish'd, all in arms,
> All plum'd like estridges that wing the wind,
> Baited like eagles having lately bathed.[1]

We do not, perhaps, realize the amount of maintenance that was necessary for troops, their armour and weapons. Untreated steel will rust in a matter of minutes under damp or foggy conditions. Hence Othello's

> Keep up your bright swords, for the dew will rust them.[2]

We must imagine the troops' work since long before dawn, with oil and sand scouring the weapons, oiling mail and breastplates. This is the

---

[1] *I Henry IV* IV.1.98. I do not accept my friend Professor A. R. Humphreys' latest Arden Edition (1960), while recognizing the estridge-difficulty and the force of the example which he quotes in his Appendix V. See also *infra*. 'with the wind' (Qq, E) seems to me rythmically awkward. There may be a secondary meaning in 'baited' = refreshed: as of travellers at an inn.
[2] I.2.59.

THE HAWK AND THE HANDSAW

simile for the army on parade, the short-winged hawks that are plum'd, preened (another spelling is *pruned*). At once we are deep in a complex of submerged metaphors, ambiguities, even puns. They are *plum'd* – their plumage *preened* – but you can see the feather crests, perhaps of ostrich, on the helmets, too. The oiled armour is shining, like the hawk's feathers. They are *baited* – the two meanings; for they have fluttered their wings and loosened their muscles for the conquering flight; they have *baited*, refreshed themselves and slept during the night's bivouac. But here are two kinds of the hawk tribe, as it were conflated in imagery; the estridges, the short-winged hawks, lithe and fierce, to fly quick and low to the attack, not to tower and stoop like the falcon; and the eagles (seldom manned for hawking, and, if they were, a royal gift between emperors), carrying from a multitude of sources – we may remember the Bible and the Roman emblem – all the connotations of fierceness, strength, swiftness, and sun-gazing power, mysterious in their ways

> They were swifter than eagles, they were stronger than lions.[1]

in the air. Professor Humphreys[2] has stressed with admirable acuteness the vividness of the passage and what follows. But the lines that follow the description seem to me sharply differentiated from the baroque imagery that expands it – Mercury, Pegasus, Mars and the rest – which seems to be 'frigid'[3] and unconvincing.

VII

There is another image, perhaps unfamiliar to many readers, requires mention. It was possible for a hawk to damage a wing-feather; either by careless handling, by 'bating', or by crashing into a branch or thicket in the attempt to follow a low-flying quarry. The damaged feather had to be repaired. During the annual moult the falconer would collect the discarded feathers. The injured feather was then cut off just above the break. A matching feather was selected and cut to length. A needle was

---

[1] *2 Samuel* 1:23. There are many allusions in the Bible, and the folk-lore is voluminous.
[2] Note to the Arden Edition, p. 124.
[3] In Longinus' sense.

then soaked in brine so as to provide a rough friction surface; one end was inserted into the pith of the old stump, the other into the new, and the two ends drawn together over the stiffening needle. This was the process known as *imping*. The word is used only once, but colloquially and with several implications (as of temporary expedients in a crisis) in *Richard II*. Ross is speaking to Northumberland of the state of England:

> If then we shall shake off our slavish yoke,
> *Imp* out our drooping country's *broken wing*,
> Redeem from broking pawn the blemish'd crown . . .[1]

The point here is not merely the violence of the transition, from the semi-cliché of 'shake off the yoke' to the larger image of 'drooping' – of the bird or country maimed by rebellion – but also the immensity of the operation in 'imping', not a single feather, but a whole series of deficiencies caused by England's domestic catastrophes and mismanagement.

The diseases of hawks were innumerable. As with most captive things their health was largely a matter of exercise and diet.[2] Two images only seem significant here. Both are spontaneous. The first is from *Measure for Measure*.

All hawks and owls that feed on birds and 'small deer' eat feathers and fur together. In the process of digestion these are gathered up into small pellets, which are disgorged by the bird. The falconer is enjoined to provide a tray of small stones, which are also 'cast'. Inspection of the 'mutes' (droppings) has to be continuous, and various medicines are prescribed for the different conditions, including (but as a last resort) cautery of the head. So the image of 'casting' or purging is used of Angelo:

> His filth within being cast, he would appear
> A pond as deep as hell.[3]

[1] II.1.292.
[2] See T. H. White, *passim*, on his difficulties with the goshawk. The diet had also to be considered most carefully in relation to the amount of 'flying time' of the bird.
[3] III.1.91. I do not think that in this context 'cast' can mean 'cast off'.

THE HAWK AND THE HANDSAW

Again we may quote Blome:

> To conclude; Concerning the giving *Stones*, you must use the *Stones* and *Castings* with discretion: The latter without the former in a *Hawk*, (supposed to be clean) will work no effect, and thereby deceive you. For Example: Give such a *Hawk* as you suppose to be very clean, *Casting* for a *week* together, and she will render it fair and white, and do but then give her some *Stones* and then *Casting*, and you shall soon find some filth and glut which the *Stones* had made fit to remove by the *Casting* . . .[1]

The 'castings' were 'sometimes *Plumage*, and sometimes knots of Flannel, or *Feather Castings*, and sometimes *Phisick*, as you see occasion by their Castings or Mutes'.[2]

This is precisely Angelo's character. He is supposed to be clean, a model of sexual purity, and has deceived the other characters. But if he could be once purged his wickedness would be revealed in all its depth. And we remember the unsavoury associations of 'pond' in *The Tempest*.

The second remarkable image is that of *enseamed*; Hamlet's term of disgust for his Mother. The images converge, as it were, from two sides:

> Queen.   O Hamlet! speak no more;
>   Thou turn'st mine eyes into my very soul;
>   And there I see such black and grained spots
>   As will not leave their tinct.
> Hamlet.   Nay, but to live
>   In the rank sweat of an *enseaméd* bed
>   *Stew'd* in corruption, *honeying* and making love
>   Over the nasty *stye* . . .[3]

The Queen's image for her soul is almost abstract, and certainly traditional, as of stained linen or sheets, ('grained' is 'engrained'). Hamlet's mind leaps, as does Leontes', to the concrete:

> Dost think I am so muddy, so unsettled,
> To appoint myself in this vexation; sully
> The purity and whiteness of my sheets

---

[1] Blome *op. cit.* p. 75.
[2] *Ibid.* p. 78.
[3] III.4.88. I see no reason whatever to read *unseamed*.

THE LIVING IMAGE

> Which to preserve is sleep; which, being spotted
> Is goads, thorns, nettles, tails of wasps?[1]

Enseamed (ensemé) is used of the condition of a hawk that has an excess of grease in her body. Blome repeatedly gives directions to 'scour and en-seame her'.[2]

> About a *Fortnight* or three *Weeks* before you intend to draw your *Hawk* out of the *Mew*, let her be fed twice a *Day* with clean drest and washt *Meat*; and you will find her thereby well advanced towards her *Enseaming*. She will likewise thereby have scowred out of her *Pannel* and *Gut*, much of that *Glut* and *Grease* which hath engendered which will prevent many dangers that might have befallen her through Heat . . .[3]

Shakespeare's use of any form of greasiness to convey repulsion from touch, smell, perhaps even taste, is well known, and linked with sexual disgust. We have the 'old greasy dishes': Cleopatra is 'a morsel cold upon/Dead Caesar's trencher'; there are the 'greasy relics' of Cressida's faith: in *Love's Labour's Lost* the Princess' 'greasy talk' is synonymous with the risqué. In the Hamlet passage the images move in a kind of vortex; the bed rank with sweat, the corruption seething like a stew (with the subsidiary sense of 'stew' as a brothel). Perhaps there is even that antique image of honey = sexual intercourse;[4] the whole converging as it were on the evil smell of the *stye*: 'this loathsome stye' of *Pericles*.

VIII

There are in existence nearly four hundred books on falconry, besides innumerable manuscripts. The theme figures constantly in pictorial art, and particularly in tapestries, up to the end of the eighteenth century. It is, and must be, a diminishing art because of the lack of open spaces on which game is preserved. At the same time there has been a peculiar revival for a specific purpose.

[1] *The Winter's Tale* 1.2.324.
[2] Blome, *op. cit.* p. 71.
[3] *Ibid.* p. 75.
[4] As in Porphyry.

THE HAWK AND THE HANDSAW

In 1851 the amenities of the Great Exhibition were endangered by multitudes of sparrows. The Duke of Wellington, being appealed to by Queen Victoria, gave the characteristically brief and sensible answer: 'Hawks, Ma'am'. A modern menace – apart from the London starlings and pigeons – is the presence of the same birds, and sometimes of seagulls, on certain airfields. As I write I have before me a description of a 'squadron' of sixteen falcons on duty on a large field in East Anglia in order to obviate or at least diminish the danger of birds being sucked into the air intake-ports of jet engines, with the certainty of damage and danger. The birds are of six species, from Africa, India and North America. The patrols fly daily from 10 a.m. to 6 p.m., 'waiting on' in the sky above the falconers in the traditional manner. Few birds are actually killed. The presence of the hawks is enough to keep them well away from the airfields.

It is not difficult to account for the extreme antiquity of hawking. We may think that it has offered a surrogate for man's aspiration towards flight, achieved with infinite grace and a fierce energy. Of all birds only the hawk can be trained to co-operate productively with the will of man. In the long and laborious process of manning a peculiar relationship is established. But the man-hawk relationship seems also to to have a sexual component. She, the female, is dominated by patient love, and some cruelty. That relationship has qualities which are peculiarly human; yet fierce, capricious, temperamental. She is to be introduced gradually to the world in which she will live:

> When she is on the *Perch* let some *Company* be discoursing or walking near at hand, that she may observe them, yet not so near as to disturb her: And when you perceive her pretty quiet, take her gently to your *Fist*, stroking her with a *Feather*. If she be troublesome and very coy, set her down again, and take her up a second time about an *hour* after, and so continue till you have gained her love . . .[1]

> You may feed within an *hour* after it, and it will make her very fond of you, full, haughty and proud . . .[2]

It was fitting that Hero finds such words for Beatrice

[1] Blome, *op. cit.* p. 73.
[2] *Ibid.* p. 87.

> I know her spirits are as coy and wild
> As haggards of the rock.[1]

Again we may quote T. H. White on the larger parable of the hawk in a turbulent world:

> A few peaks of human achievement would survive: peaks of patience and conquest by culture . . . Since China, since Assyria, but not since Hitler or Stalin, man had reconciled the eagle.[2]

[1] *Much Ado* III.1.35.
[2] White, *op. cit.* p. 72.

CHAPTER 3

The Ritual of the Hunt

I

The Elizabethan hunt had aspects that were both ritual, utilitarian, and aesthetic. The aristocratic and precise language of its many phases was traditional from Norman times. The careful pre-selection of the quarry to be hunted was designed, not only to afford the superior sport to be obtained from a beast 'of the first water' and to ensure excellent condition for the venison, but to keep the herd in the best possible state as a source of food. It was *not* 'the pursuit of the inedible by the unmentionable'. The fox was then, and for many years afterwards, vermin, and the thought of pursuing the 'carted' Exmoor stag would have been unthinkable. The ritual included complicated traditional horn-music for the different stages of the chase; full directions are given in *The Master of Game*[1] and elsewhere. But aesthetically the chief pleasure was the hound-music. There are complex aspects of this.

The full cry of a pack of hounds is a music that is both exciting and mysterious. It has affinities with the cry of wild geese in flight, with the curlew's 'sweet crystalline cry'. It is associated in folklore with the Wild Hunt, Gabriel's Hounds, the *cwn annwn* that presage death and disaster.[2] It is this music that the Elizabethans valued. A passage from *A Midsummer Night's Dream* will serve as a starting point.

Theseus and Hyppolyta with their train have come across the sleeping lovers in assorted uncomfortable (though chaste) positions. Theseus orders the huntsmen to wake them with their horns.[3] They have per-

---

[1] A translation of *Livre de Chasse* by Gaston de Foix.
[2] See E. A. Armstrong, *The Folklore of Birds*, p. 217ff.
[3] I have read of this form of reveillé in hunting circles in France today: the huntsman being engaged to make music under his master's windows. So, on occasion, with bagpipes in Scotland.

41

formed the May Day rites, the 'observation'. Then Theseus:

> Go, one of you, find out the forester;
> For now our observation is perform'd;
> And since we have the vaward of the day,
> My love shall hear the music of my hounds.
> Uncouple in the western valley; let them go:
> Dispatch, I say, and find the forester.
> We will, fair queen, up to the mountain's top,
> And mark the musical confusion
> Of hounds and echo in conjunction.[1]

The party is, presumably, on the slopes of a hill in an English park rather than a mountain in 'A Wood near Athens'. The forester and his assistants were responsible for knowing exactly where each 'warrantable' (fit for hunting) beast might be feeding (pasturing) and lying up at night in a thicket or coppice. On the previous day, or in the very early morning, he would have made quite sure of the hart's position by tracking it to the thicket with *lymers* or lyme-hounds, in appearance something like bloodhounds, distinguished for their powers of scenting. He would have worked them, of course, on a leash, to make certain that the hart was not prematurely roused, merely marked down; and he would stand by the thicket, watching and waiting for orders. These came when the house-party, lords and ladies, probably on horseback, had taken up their position on some commanding high ground, on the knoll that we so often find in an Elizabethan park; or, as Theseus did, on a convenient mountain side. All knew that the hart would circle round them, as a beast usually does in hilly country. When they were in position the order would be sent to the huntsman to find the forester, bring his hounds to where the hart was harboured, and 'uncouple' to start the hunt.

But let us go back to Theseus and Hippolyta on the hill-top: grouped, on their horses, drinking in the morning air. Theseus has just boasted about *his* hounds; but Hippolyta, the virgin huntress, isn't going to let him get away with it. So she proceeds to boast in her turn, with a hint of emulous malice:

[1] *Midsummer Night's Dream* IV.I.105.

THE RITUAL OF THE HUNT

> I was with Hercules and Cadmus once
> When in a wood of Crete they bay'd the bear
> With hounds of Sparta: never did I hear
> Such gallant chiding; for, besides the groves
> The skies, the fountains, every region near
> Seem'd all one mutual cry. I never heard
> So musical a discord, such sweet thunder.

Theseus is obviously offended at the implied slight on his pack: so he replies (and how magnificently the verse clamours, like hound voices themselves):

> My hounds are bred out of the Spartan kind,
> So flew'd, so sanded, and their heads are hung
> With ears that sweep away the *m*orning dew
> Slow in pursuit but *m*atched in *m*outh like bells
> Each under each. A cry more tuneable
> Was never holla'd to, nor cheer'd with horn,
> In Crete, in Sparta, nor in Thessaly:
> Judge, when you hear.[1]

When someone, perhaps an A.D.C., had established contact with the forester patiently watching the thicket or coppice where the warrantable hart was 'harboured', the huntsman would proceed to rouse the stag by drawing, as we should say, the covert with his hounds. The pack would have been halted some distance from the harbour, so as not to disturb the hart prematurely. When the huntsman had moved the hart, he blew on his horn: the technical bugle or horn call known as a *recheat*. This consisted of a four-note call, followed by an interval, repeated three times. If the stag broke away, but the huntsman didn't see him, he blew the *recheat* only; if he saw the stag break, he blew not only the *recheat* but the *moot* as well: and the *moot* was a single note, long or short, the rough equivalent of the modern 'Gone Away!'. That seems to be the explanation of an exceptionally difficult passage in *Much Ado* when Benedick says (labouring the inevitable pun on cuckoldry):

[1] IV.I.121.

THE LIVING IMAGE

–but that I will have a recheat winded in my
forehead, or hang my bugle in an invisible baldrick,
all women shall pardon me.[1]

II

But the music of the hounds was the real point: they were bred for their mouths, not only for their toughness and nose. Further, the Elizabethan pack had none of that uniformity of appearance and 'throat' that we look for today. For it had to be of mixed 'voice',[2] and we have directions from Gaston de Foix as to how you should compound your kennel for 'sweetness of cry': with bass, tenor, counter-tenor and trebles. These last were what we should now call terriers: so that there were big dogs and little dogs together. There were the running hounds, some of them with 'hairy tails', greyhounds, and the greyhound type called an *alaunt*.[3] And because it was essential that they should run more or less together (even to the proverbial table-cloth today) it was necessary to *trash* the bigger dogs – attach a weight, or add a weighted leash to their collars, to hold them back. That is the point of Prospero's remark that he came to know which of his courtiers

to trash for overtopping.[4]

For it was not only the disparity in size but over-eagerness in individual hounds that might easily cause the pack to become dispersed, and in a woodland where there were many deer such roving hounds would cause infinite trouble, distracting attention from the chosen quarry. And nothing was, and is, worse than for the huntsman (particularly in woodland) to lose control of some of his hounds. Therefore such hounds were *trashed*: that is they had heavily-weighted leads attached

---

[1] 1.1.250.
[2] Sir Roger de Coverley, we are told, refused the gift of a hound on the grounds that its voice would not harmonize with his own pack (*Spectator*, No. 116, 1711).
[3] *Master of Game* Chs. XIV–XVI.
[4] *Tempest* 1.2.81.

THE RITUAL OF THE HUNT

to their collars to slow them down.[1] Iago (*Othello* is rich in hound-imagery) puns execrably with reference to Roderigo's general character:

> Which thing to do
> If this poor trash of Venice, whom I trash
> For his quick hunting, stand the putting-on,
> I'll have our Michael Cassio on the hip.[2]

Roderigo himself is poor-spirited, self-pitying in his hound-like propensities, never quite realizing his ambitions, always behind the course of events:

> I do follow here in the chase, not like a hound that hunts, but one that fills up the cry.[3]

Shakespeare's attitude to dogs is ambivalent. They are often emblems of cowardice, betrayal, as in *Lear*:

> The little dogs and all,
> Tray, Blanch and Sweet-heart, see, they bark at me.[4]

Both the spaniel and the greyhound are usually, though not invariably, types of fawning sycophancy, and the verb *spaniel'd* is a brilliant image:

> The hearts
> That spaniel'd me at heels, to whom I gave
> Their wishes, do discandy, melt their sweets
> On blossoming Caesar;[5]

I think that Rylands[6] was the first to point out the inwardness of this image; the dogs beneath the table licking the fingers of the courtiers who had been eating sweetmeats. Both Blome and *The Master of Game* have much to say about spaniels; and it is perhaps not unduly meta-

---

[1] This may be sometimes seen today with sheep-dogs: a billet of wood hung from their collars so as to knock against their forelegs, in order to slow them down.
[2] *Othello* II.1.312.
[3] *Othello* II.3.360: i.e. contributing to the 'music' but ineffective in the pursuit.
[4] III.6.62.
[5] *Antony and Cleopatra* IV.10.33.
[6] *Words and Poetry*, London, 1928.

45

physical to perceive a contrast between their servility and the pride of the hawks for which they roused the game from the stubbles or undergrowth.

Launce's dog Crab lives on in *The Two Gentlemen of Verona*: Rabelaisian, poker-faced, a born comedian. There is Lady the Brach who appears, curiously, twice, as if she were some remembered animal. There are Prospero's hounds in *The Tempest*:

> *Enter divers spirits in shape of hounds, and hunt them about, Prospero and Ariel setting them on.*
>
> *Prospero.* Hey, Mountain, hey!
> *Ariel.* Silver, there it goes, Silver!
> *Prospero.* Fury, Fury! there, Tyrant, there! hark, hark!
> (Caliban, Stephano and Trinculo are driven out.)[1]

Silver the hound also occurs in *The Taming of the Shrew*, in a notable passage; the Lord is talking to his First Huntsman:

> Huntsman, I charge thee, tender well my hounds:
> Brach Merriman, the poor cur, is emboss'd,
> And couple Clowder with the deep-mouth'd brach.
> Saw'st thou not, boy, how Silver made it good
> At the hedge-corner, in the coldest fault?
> I would not lose the dog for twenty pound.[2]

Merriman is *embossed*, utterly worn-out with the hunt, perhaps foaming at the mouth. The term is also used of horses and of bears. Clowder is to sire the puppies of the 'deep-mouthed brach'; again the concern for hound-music. Silver has a specially good nose. So has Sowter of *Twelfth Night*: Fabian dragging him in gratuitously (but in a reflex response to Sir Toby's jest about the 'cold scent' while Malvolio is puzzling out the letters):

> Sowter will cry upon't, . . . though it be as rank as a fox.[3]

[1] IV.1.252.
[2] Induction 1.16.
[3] II.5.130. 'Cry on't' – acknowledge the true trail when it has been broken – the 'coldest fault'.

THE RITUAL OF THE HUNT

We may note the extreme accuracy (and depth) of the simile. Malvolio is as it were sniffing round the riddle of the letters, casting this way and that, shuffling M, O, A, I in his mind. Sowter, a notable hound, is able to pick out the cold scent, even though the trail has been crossed by a fox, the beast of 'stinking flight'.

Other hounds have their vices. One of the most exasperating, as every dog-trainer knows, is that of hunting a trail backwards instead of forwards; the game getting further and further away as he does so. This is the point of Falstaff's contemptuous

> You hunt counter: hence! avaunt![1]

and

> How cheerfully on the false trail they cry!
> O this is counter, you false Danish dogs![2]

Once the image is compounded, as it were, so as to clog our response:

> A hound that runs counter, and yet draws dry-foot well[3]

for 'drawing dry foot' was the unusual ability to follow the trail of the deer when the scent was minimal, working from the 'slot' or hoofprint.

The dialogue of the *Induction* goes on:

> 1 Hun. Why, Bellman is as good as he, my lord;
> He cried upon it at the merest loss,
> And twice today pick'd out the dullest scent:
> Trust me, I take him for the better dog.
> Lord. Thou art a fool: if Echo were as fleet,
> I would esteem him worth a dozen such.

But the Lord, or the playhouse copyist, or the compositor of the First Folio, has gone wrong, for *Merriman* must be the name of a *dog* hound, not of a bitch, and *brach* means bitch. Dyce, followed by Madden, suggests *Trash* Merriman, weighted by a strap at the collar. But Merriman, poor brute, is already *embossed* – flanks heaving, foam at the

---

[1] *2 Henry IV* I.2.91.
[2] *Hamlet* IV.5.106.
[3] *Comedy of Errors* IV.2.39. See *Shakespeare's England*, II, p. 335-6.

jaws. To have him *trashed* would have been the act of a lunatic. Dover Wilson suggests *broach* (to let blow) which seems to me an improbable emendation. I suggest, tentatively,

Mark Merriman . . .

or

Brave Merriman . . .

instead of the *Brach* of the normal text.

So we have a sort of catalogue of Shakespeare's hounds: Bellman, Echo, Mountain, Ringwood, Fury, Silver, Sowter.[1] Madden pointed out that these are still hound names in kennels (though I have not heard of Sowter) and we are all familiar with John Peel.[2] We need not wonder at the conservatism. Huntsmen and kennelmen today must know all their hounds by name, and the hounds must respond. But in order to call a name aloud it must be short (usually not above two syllables) and have qualities of pitch and tone to which a dog will respond. This limits the choice, and names are handed down through the hound-generations.

III

The Boke of St. Albans (XII) contains high praise of the hare,

that beest king of all venery

and has some curious things to say about it, for it was believed to vary its sex from time to time. The two methods of hunting were coursing with greyhounds, and pursuit with what we should now call harriers. The images from both are widespread throughout the plays. Greyhounds straining at the leash provide the images of troops eager for war in *Coriolanus*,[3] *Henry V*,[4] *I Henry IV*.[5] The great venue for coursing was Cotswold, and its matches were celebrated: Page's fallowed grey-

---

[1] *The Boke of St. Albans* adds the names of *Richer* and *Bemounde* (XII).
[2] His 'Ruby' and 'Ranter' supplement Shakespeare's.
[3] 1.6.37.
[4] *Chorus*, 6, and III.1.30.
[5] 1.3.278.

THE RITUAL OF THE HUNT

hound was outrun there. A recent work[1] describes the Games and their history. The hare had first to be found in her form (see p. 13 *supra*) for the pun, and the finder is enjoined to cry 'So ho!'. This is the verbal trigger for Mercutio:

> *Nurse.* If you be he, sir, I desire some confidence in you.
> *Benvolio.* She will indite him to some supper.
> *Mercutio.* A bawd, a bawd, a bawd! So ho!
> *Romeo.* What hast thou found?
> *Mercutio.* No hare, sir; unless a hare sir, in a lenten pie, that is something stale and hoar ere it be spent.
>   An old hare hoar, and an old hare hoar
>   Is very good meat in Lent:
>   But a hare that is hoar, is too much for a score,
>   When it hoars ere it be spent.[2]

The obscene wit of Mercutio's comment may require explanation. The Nurse invites Romeo to dinner: Mercutio promptly takes it as an invitation to a bawdy-house. *Bawd* is still used in Scotland for a hare. Mercutio's 'So ho!' recognizes that he has perceived the girl whom he thinks the Nurse is offering. Romeo caps it with

> What hast thou found?

i.e. the responding to the hare-finder's call. Mercutio comes back with his bawdy snatch, which turns on the rutting madness of hares in March and their proverbial zeal in procreation.[3] It drew from Dr. Johnson the celebrated (and not unjustified) comment: 'a series of quibbles unworthy of explanation, which he who does not understand need not lament his ignorance'. And today we should include in the same condemnation the puns on deer-horns (cuckolds); harts – hearts; again, Johnson: 'He is not long without some idle conceit, or contemptible equivocation'.

The judgement of the outcome of the coursing, the triumphs of the 'swallow-footed greyhound' was governed then as now, by a system of

---

[1] *Robert Dover and the Cotswold Games – Annalia Dubrensia*, ed. Christopher Whitford, London 1962.
[2] *Romeo and Juliet* II.4.130.
[3] They are linked with goats, a standard image for lust, in *Cymbeline* IV.4.37.

THE LIVING IMAGE

points, each with technical name. There was the 'turn', the 'go by', the 'wrench', the 'cote' and finally the 'taking' of the hare. The 'cote' was the passing of the other greyhound of the leash: Rosencrantz and Guildernstern 'coted' the Players on their way to Elsinore.[1] So William Denny:[2]

> The swallow-footed greyhound hath the prize,
> A silver-studded collar, who outflies
> The rest in lightning's speed, who first comes by
> His strayning copes-mates, with celerity
> Turnes his affrighted game, then coates againe
> His forward rivall, on the senceless plaine,
> And after laborinthian turnes, surprise
> The game, while he doth pant her obsequies.

For taking hares on any large scale, and in condition fit for food, the normal method was to drive them into 'toils' or nets like those used for deer: the nets being loosely hung on twigs set across her 'meuses'[3] or runs. Hares keep year after year to these tracks, which may well pass through gateways, or gaps in hedges. Shakespeare calls the hare 'purblind', and at certain times, notably during the March madness, they will run between a spectator's legs without any signs of fear.

But the harrier pack, the beagles 'so small that they may be carried in a man's glove', provided sport for the poor man because the hunt might so easily be followed on foot. The beagles were 'of curious scents, and passing cunning in their hunting; for the most part tyring (but seldom killing) the prey except at some strange advantage'.[4] There is a pack of beagles in *Timon of Athens*, and this is not improbable, for beagling is mentioned (along with coursing) by Arrian. Timon dismisses Alcibiades:

> Get thee away, and take
> Thy beagles with thee.[5]

[1] *Hamlet* II.2.330.
[2] William Denny: in *Robert Dover and the Cotswold Games*, p. 116 (also quoted by Madden).
[3] 'musets' in the famous description in *Venus and Adonis* (l.683).
[4] Gervase Markham, *Country Contentments*.
[5] IV.3.176. The reference is contemptuous.

50

THE RITUAL OF THE HUNT

Beagles work slowly, puzzling out the line, for 'Poor Wat' of *Venus and Adonis* had many tricks: doubling back, going among sheep or rabbits or deer to confuse the scent. During the numerous checks the beagles would cast sideways, find the line, lose and regain it by their pertinacity. Spectators on foot could easily keep up with them; particularly as a hare will frequently run in irregular circles, returning to the spot from which she was first started. The most famous simile is that used by Sir Toby Belch, who had clearly done much hunting:

> *Sir Andrew.* Beshrew me, she's a good wench.
> *Sir Toby.* She's a beagle, true-bred, and one that adores me: what o' that?[1]

The speeches seem to characterize the two knights. Sir Andrew is dull and rather stupid. Sir Toby seizes on an expressive image. Maria is stocky, strong, pert, eager and gay; alluding perhaps also to her ability to provide sport in the gulling of Malvolio.

IV

Turberville in *The Noble Art of Venerye* is rather contemptuous of fox-hunting, speaking of fox and badger and such like as vermin. Venus advises Adonis to pursue the hare, roe or fox rather than the dangerous wild boar, at whose tusks he finally meets his death. The fox 'lived by subtlety'. In *The Merry Wives* the search for Falstaff is described in terms of a fox-hunt, the way of escape having been first stopped, as earths are stopped today. The image in *King Lear* seems to be the Biblical one, from the exploits of Samson:

> He that parts us shall bring a brand from heaven,
> And fire us hence like foxes.[2]

Edgar's animal catalogue includes 'hog in sloth, fox in stealth, wolf in greediness, dog in madness, lion in prey'.[3] Perhaps the only notable image is that in which the exasperated Duke of *Twelfth Night* dismisses Viola for what he assumes to be her perfidy:

[1] *Twelfth Night* II.3.182. Folio reads *Before me*, which is possible.
[2] V.3.22. v. *Judges* 15.4.
[3] III.4.90.

THE LIVING IMAGE

> O thou dissembling cub! what wilt thou be
> When time hath sow'd a grizzle on thy case?[1]

– where the 'case' is the 'term of art' for a fox's skin. This gives some point to the bad pun in *The Winter's Tale*:

> Though my case be a pitiful one, I hope I shall not be flayed out of it.[2]

I do not know whether the badger was pursued by the Elizabethans for anything except its skin; Shakespeare does not mention it.[3]

V

In the Forest of Fontainebleau we come across, at the junctions of certain rides or avenues, open spaces in which circular low tables are built, with grooves cut in them. A large central one is for the king, the smaller ones for courtiers and noblemen; for it was a convention that the king's 'tale of slain' must be larger than that of anyone else. Hunting on the continent was remarkable for the numbers killed. Sacheverell Sitwell notes that the two Electors of Saxony, during the seventy years of their joint reigns (1611–1681) killed 110,530 deer and 52,400 wild boars, besides wolves and bears.[4] The ritual Elizabethan hunt does not seem to have worked on anything like this scale. But from time to time there were mass slaughters, like the modern *battue*, at which considerable quantities of animals were killed: when a 'feast was toward' in castle or manor. The deer would have been killed by being driven into 'toils', loose-hung nets, or shot as they went past a tryst or in a *cul-de-sac*.[5] In some forest clearing, or on the stone tables of Fontainebleau, the deer were piled or laid out. This was called the quarry, from the French *curée*: it was originally the mess of oatmeal and entrails given to the hounds *sur le cuir*, on the flayed hide of the beast.

[1] V.1.167.
[2] IV.3.825.
[3] There are several references in *Exodus* to badger-skins for the tent covering the Ark.
[4] *The Hunters and the Hunted*, p. 57.
[5] Machine-guns are sometimes used by modern deer-poachers in Scotland.

THE RITUAL OF THE HUNT

So Ross brings the news of the murder by Macbeth of Macduff's wife and children:

> Your castle is surprised, your wife and babes
> Savagely slaughtered; to relate the manner
> Were, on the quarry of these murdered deer,
> To add the death of you.[1]

Even more famous is Fortinbras' comment on the dead bodies that litter the stage at the end of *Hamlet*:

> This quarry cries on havoc. O proud death!
> What feast is toward in thine eternal cell
> That thou so many princes at a blow
> So bloodily has struck?[2]

Coriolanus' mind runs on a pile of bodies of the plebeians:

> Would the nobility lay aside their ruth
> And let me use my sword, I'd make a quarry
> With thousands of these quarter'd slaves, as high
> As I could pick my lance.[3]

There is the possibility of confusion between this sense of the heap of bodies (the normal one in Shakespeare) and the present archaic sense of any animal that is pursued in the hunt.

VI

But the ritual, and the rhythm, of the hunt seems to have some elements of a kind of miniature tragedy. In that rhythm we have the ceremonious preparation; the horns in the woodland, the music; the mysterious archetypal imagery of the pack,[4] the nobility of the victim; the sacrificial death of the One against the Many; the despatch by the sword of the animal at bay; and what has been called 'the infinite serene of No

---

[1] IV.3.204. Presumably there is a faint resonance of the standard pun, even on such an occasion, of *deer – dear*.
[2] V.2.364. 'Cries on havoc': calls out for revenge.
[3] I.1.199.
[4] Such as the huntsman and his hounds, for Death.

Retreat' The consummation in death is a ritual. There is fear in the picture of the savaging boar. His charge, met with the spear, is a common emblem of war. There is fear, exaltation, and a measure of pity. Behind lies much history and myth: the archetype of man's life and its pursuit of the hounds of time, or death, or lust, or guilt: the Eumenides, Actaeon, Dido, the tapestries of the Renaissance: the Wild Hunt with their ghostly riders and packs, whose baying is answered by earthly dogs. Armstrong[1] points out that owl, raven, ban-dogs and wolves are linked in Shakespeare's mind.

We seem to have (as so often) this curious ambivalence: the freshness of the countryside when

> The hunt is up, the morn is bright and grey,
> The fields are fragrant and the woods are green . . .[2]

against the scene of the hart – itself numinous, perhaps, through St. Hubert's Cross – at bay in water or against a cliff, the sword thrust, the merciful blow, the dispersion of strength. We may not underestimate the appeal of the chase: we do well not to neglect its images as parables.

> Some day we shall get up before the dawn
> And find our ancient hounds before the door,
> And wide awake know that the hunt is on;
> Stumbling upon the blood-dark track once more,
> Then stumbling to the kill beside the shore;
> Then cleaning out and bandaging of wounds,
> And chants of victory amid the encircling hounds.[3]

[1] *Shakespeare's Imagination*, p. 233.
[2] *Titus Andronicus* II.2.1.
[3] W. B. Yeats, 'Hound Voice'.

CHAPTER 4

'The pleasant'st angling'

I

The imagery that Shakespeare drew from fishing is not, I think, remarkable. In comparison with that which derives from hawking, hunting, horsemanship it seems flat and formalized, used in a somewhat deliberate and abstract fashion. The allusions were gathered up a century ago by The Rev. Henry N. Ellacombe,[1] at a period when such peripheral monographs were common: Shakespeare the Seaman, Shakespeare the Botanist, Shakespeare (this was indeed a crop of dragons' teeth) the Lawyer. Nor do we find any vivid imagery connected with lakes or rivers; even the sea-imagery seems, on the whole, 'frigid'.

We may account for this. Hunting and hawking, and horsemanship, were traditionally aristocratic pursuits. They were closely linked to war, diplomacy, and the country gentleman's recreations: they involved the traditional manly qualities of Castiglione's *Courtier*. They were also involved to a greater or lesser degree with the country people, from whom, through the entourage of the Great House, they would have drawn many auxiliaries. One result, as I have pointed out, was a widespread and spontaneous knowledge of the sport: we may suggest some analogy with Irish fox-hounds and harriers today.[2]

Fishing with rod and line was by comparison a solitary and rather static pursuit. It offered no parables of war, it contained no challenges to robust manhood.[3] It played no part in the household economy; the

---

[1] *Antiquary*, Vol. IV, 1881: *Gentleman's Magazine*, 1895. (*cit.* Madden).
[2] See, *e.g.* Somerville and Ross, 'A Patrick's Day Hunt', *Some Irish Yesterdays*, 1906: and the once-popular novels of Dorothea Conyers (*fl.* 1900–10). In England, participation is much more limited.
[3] Although there is one allusion to salmon fishing as a test of 'hardihood and strength.'

Great House, like the religious foundations, had its fish-ponds for Lent. Popular iconography still credits the monks with fishing for this purpose. These would have contained, like those of Chaucer's Franklin, bream and pike, with probably carp and tench, rudd or roach as well as eels. They would be taken when required with nets, or perhaps by draining individual ponds. The bream and roach would indeed have required religious fortitude to make them into articles of food; tench and pike are relatively palatable. And the luce or pike was borne in the coat of arms of Sir Thomas Lucy of Charlecote; a good example of punning heraldry.[1]

The Avon at Stratford contained only coarse fish – pike, bream roach, pevel, chub, dace, carp. A trout stream, the River Dene, runs through Charlecote Park that belonged to Sir Thomas Lucy. Trout in such a stream would be difficult to net, and highly prized for eating. It is possible that trout-fishing, here as elsewhere, was jealously guarded as the author of *The Arte of Angling* (anon. 1577) seems to suggest:

> I dare not well deal in the angling of the trout, for displeasing of one of our wardens, which either is counted the best trouter in England, or so thinketh, who would not (as I suppose) have the taking of that fish common. But yet thus much I may say, that he worketh with a fly in a box.[2]

There were not many 'books of sport' dealing with fishing that were available to Shakespeare; and there is not the slightest evidence that he ever knew them. The most important was *The Treatyse of Fysshinge with an Angle* by Dame Juliana Berners, included in the second (1496) edition of *The Boke of St. Albans*, but believed to have been written half a century before. All subsequent writers on fishing have plagiarised each other steadily and without shame. Leonard Mascall pirated Dame Juliana's work in 1590 under the title of *A Booke of Fishing with Hooke and Line* (1590). There was also *The Secrets of Angling* (1713). Salmon fishing was only made practicable by the invention of the reel and running line in the second half of the seventeenth century.

---

[1] See in particular Leslie Hotson, *Shakespeare vs Shallow*. London, 1931.
[2] p. 64: in the Princeton Facsimile of 1956. Presumably the reference is to flies stored in a box, though it is not impossible that he meant a box in which live insects were kept, for dapping.

'THE PLEASANT'ST ANGLING'

II

Fishing with rod and line for the coarse fish of the Avon or of the Huntingdonshire Ouse (the scene of *The Arte of Angling*) was a peaceful and solitary recreation. *Piscator* of that book writes of

> that pleasure that I have always most recreated myself withal, and had most delight in, and is most meetest for a solitary man and is also of light cost.[1]

It involved the exercise of certain qualities which were unlike those of the hunter. The passage is so delightful as to deserve quotation in full. It is in part a parody of the Christian cardinal virtues, and he is moralizing to his pupil:

> 1. He must have faith, believing that there is fish where he cometh to angle. 2. He must have hope that they will bite. 3. Love to the owner of the game. (*i.e.* he must respect fishing rights). 4. Also patience, if they will not bite, or any mishap cometh by losing of the fish, hook, or otherwise. 5. Humility to stoop, if need be to kneel or lie down on his belly, as you did today. 6. Fortitude, with manly courage, to deal with the biggest that cometh. 7. Knowledge adjoined to wisdom, to devise all manner of ways how to make them bite and to find the fault. 8. Liberality in the feeding of them. 9. A content mind with a sufficient mess, yea, and though you go home without.[2] 10. Also he must use prayer, knowing that it is God that doth bring both fowl to the net and fish to the bait. 11. Fasting he may not be offended withal, but acquaint himself with it, if it be from morning till night, to abide and to seek for the bite. 12. Also he must do alms deeds; that is to say if he meet a sickly poor body or doth know any such in the parish that would be glad of a few fishes to make a little broth withal (as often times is desired of sick persons), then he may not stick to send some or altogether. And if he have none, yet with all diligence that may [be, he] try with his angle to get some for the diseased person. 13. The last point of all the inward gifts that doth belong to an angler, is memory, that is, that he forget nothing at home when he settes out, nor anything behind him at his return.[3]

---

[1] p.31.
[2] We may remember R. L. Stevenson's *Fables* ('The Poor Thing'): 'And when the fish came to his hook in the mid-waters, he blessed God without weighing.'
[3] pp. 32, 33.

THE LIVING IMAGE

We may complete the picture by quoting a fragment of the dialogue that gives the point of view of the fisherman's wife, Cisley:

Victor. . . . Now, mistress, is it true that your husband hath caught the colic with fishing?

Cisley. Surely I suppose so, with his long standing, long fasting, and coldness of his feet, yea and sometimes sitting on the cold ground, for all is one to him, whether he catch or not catch. Yea and sometimes he cometh home with the colic, indeed, and is not well of [for] two or three days after, so that I hope he will give it over shortly.[1]

III

But in Shakespeare the references are mainly sexual. We may quote from *Antony and Cleopatra* on the Nile:

> Give me mine angle; we'll to the river; there –
> My music playing far off – I will betray
> Tawny-finn'd fishes: my bended hook shall pierce
> Their slimy jaws; and as I draw them up,
> I'll think them every one an Antony,
> And say, 'Ah, ha! you're caught'.[2]

Charmian, ever ready to pick up her mistress's mood, continues:

> 'Twas merry when
> You wagered on your angling; when your diver
> Did hang a salt-fish on his hook, which he
> With fervency drew up.[3]

Nell Gwynn, it will be remembered, played the same traditional trick on Charles II when they decided to go fishing in the Thames after an all-night party. As to Shakespeare, we may pause to suggest the shadow of a bawdy pun, which has some precedents, on salt-fish and their smell. Trinculo's comments on Caliban are relevant.[4] But one of the best-

---

[1] p. 36.
[2] II.5.11. 'Angle' is the gear in general, probably a hand-line. I do not know the fish of the Nile; perch and tiger-fish are famous.
[3] II.5.15. Ridley (Arden) gives the source from Nashe's *Lenten Stuffs*.
[4] *Tempest* II.2.25.

'THE PLEASANT'ST ANGLING'

known allusions is that from *Much Ado*:

> The pleasant'st angling is to see the fish
> Cut with her golden oars the silver stream,
> And greedily devour the treacherous bait;
> So angle we for Beatrice.[1]

The fish described might be roach, rudd, or perch. But the description is frigid (to use Longinus' term), overloaded with adjectives of the stock eighteenth century poetic diction. It recalls, perhaps, a well known passage in *The Compleat Angler*:

> ... there I sat viewing the silver streams glide slowly towards their centre, the tempestuous sea ...

which we may contrast with some stanzas from Donne's *The Baite*:

> There will the river whispering runne
> Warm'd by thy eyes, more than the Sunne,
> And there the inamored fish will stay,
> Begging themselves they may betray.
>
> When thou wilt swimme in that live bath,
> Each fish, which every channell hath,
> Will amorously to thee swimme,
> Gladder to catch thee, than thou him.

IV

But one of the most remarkable images is that used, reflectively and priggishly, by Angelo in *Measure for Measure*:

> O cunning enemy that, to catch a saint
> With saints dost bait thy hook.[2]

Walton adduces (among many authorities for the antiquity of angling) the two mentions of hooks in the Bible, in *Amos*[3] and *Job*,[4] but,

---

[1] III.1.26.
[2] II.2.180. For the general idea of this kind of deception, see *2 Corinthians*, 11:14: 'for Satan himself is transformed into an angel of light'.
[3] 4:2.
[4] 41:4.

strangely, omitting *St. Matthew*.[1] It is the passage from *Job* that is relevant here:

> Cans't thou draw out leviathan with a hook? or his tongue with a cord which thou lettest down?
> Cans't thou put an hook into his nose? or bore his jaw through with a thorn?

This and the succeeding verses caused the early commentators on the Book of Job to recognize Leviathan as typifying Satan. There was substantial evidence: the terrible teeth, the flames coming from his mouth, smoke from his nostrils, the deep sea that boiled as he passed. Clearly he was uncatchable by any ordinary means. So we get the gloss of Honorius of Autun:

> Leviathan the monster who swims in the sea of the world, is Satan. God threw the line into the sea. The Cord of the line is the human descent of Christ, the bait is His divinity. Attracted by the smell of flesh Leviathan tries to seize but the hook tears his jaws.

I have taken this account from Emile Mâle's *The Gothic Image*. With the same passage Mâle reproduces a miniature in the *Hortus Deliciarum*.[2] God is fishing with a comparatively modern-looking rod, which is bending under the weight of its bait. The line is formed of linked medallions of the Kings of Judah, and ends in the crucifix on which Christ is nailed. But the upright of the Cross ends in a kind of sharkhook; Leviathan has already mouthed the bait, and the hook has pierced his jaws. We may also remember the early Christian icon in which the anchor, the symbol of hope, serves also to suggest the crucifix: two fishes (the fish being the anagram in Greek for Christ) are impaled on the anchor flukes.

Angelo's image may also recall the method of fishing for the afancq, a monster with elements of both crocodile and hippopotamus, said to frequent lonely tarns in Wales. Here the method is to secure a stout chain to some boulder or tree near the water's edge, and to bait a large

---

[1] 17:27.
[2] 1961 (Fontana) Edition, p. 380.

'THE PLEASANT'ST ANGLING'

hook with a virgin: that is, Isabella. We may also remember Dylan Thomas' poem 'Ballad of the Long-Legged Bait'.[1]

V

But the sole image from angling that seems to me to be used with spontaneity and conviction is the sexual one. We have already seen in *The Arte of Angling* the suggestion that trout streams were carefully and jealously preserved; as opposed to the open waters like the Avon which contained only coarse fish. One reason, no doubt, was the pleasure of the sport of fly-fishing which, though starting with *The Boke of St. Albans*, was to develop steadily during the seventeenth century. Owners were jealous over the trout-streams because, besides the superior qualities of the 'meat', there was the difficulty of catching the fish other than by the orthodox and conspicuous means of rod and line, with fly or worm. Clear and shallow streams do not lend themselves to netting. The poacher had therefore only one resource, that of 'groping' or 'tickling'. This is what Lucio means when he replies to Mistress Overdone's question

> But what's his offence?
> – Groping for trouts in a peculiar [i.e. preserved] river.[2]

and gives point to Maria's

> Here comes the trout that must be caught with tickling.[3]

Since it is improbable that the reader has ever practised this form of poaching, it is as well to describe it.

Tickling is only practicable with trout of a reasonable size, say ten inches or upwards. The fish must be spotted, lying in relatively shallow water, preferably under a bank or in the shelter of a large stone; and close to the water's edge. The 'tickler', having bared his arm to the shoulder, crawls up inch by inch until he is just behind the fish. Equally slowly – for the slightest hasty movement will cause alarm – he puts his

[1] *Collected Poems* 1934–1952, p. 149.
[2] *Measure for Measure* I.2.91.
[3] *Twelfth Night* II.5.21.

arm into the water, and brings his hand up from behind under the belly of the fish. With his fingers he then starts to stroke it, with the lightest of touches, between the gills and the vent, in a delicate and slow rhythmical motion. The trout will evince signs of pleasure, and will gradually rise nearer and nearer to the surface of the water. When it is near the top of the water it can be thrown on to the bank with a quick flick of the hand.

We need not labour the sexual aspects of this; they have been noted by Eric Partridge.[1] But the image seems to me to be the only one of the angling language that is used both spontaneously and with precise implications. It might even be thought to dovetail with the legend of the deer-poaching in the park at Charlecote; similar visits to the River Dene are not incredible.

There is a final example of this sexual association. Leontes, alone with Mamillius, is at the height of his senseless fit of jealousy:

> There have been,
> Or I am much deceiv'd, cuckolds ere now;
> And many a man there is even at this present,
> Now, while I speak this, holds his wife by the arm,
> That little thinks she has been sluic'd in's absence,
> And his pond fish'd by his next neighbour, by
> Sir Smile, his neighbour: nay, there's comfort in't,
> Whiles other men have gates, and those gates opened
> As mine, against their will.[2]

The sense is plain: the image-clusters[3] seem to be working, as usual, by linked associations: *sluices, fishpond, opened gates*. All are more complex than they appear at first sight.

The 'gates' image is sexual; we need go no further than *Canticles* or Spenser's *Prothalamion* for examples. 'Sluic'd' may mean either dragging the pond with a net, or opening a sluice of a particular pond so that it is drained, and the fish easily captured. This is often the practice in a modern fish-farm. It is recorded that James I had fishponds 'on a parcel of ground within the vine-gardens at Westminster, which for the better bringing up

---

[1] *Shakespeare's Bawdy*.
[2] *Winter's Tale* I.2.190.
[3] See, generally, Armstrong, *Shakespeare's Imagination*.

'THE PLEASANT'ST ANGLING'

of the said cormorants, aspreys and otters for His Majesty's desport he had taken a lease for four years'. A house was to be built and a sluice made from the Thames to supply water to the ponds which were to be stocked with fish. We know nothing more about this. Were the cormorants, ospreys and otters kept merely for the pleasure of watching them taking the fish? Or is it conceivable that some traveller had brought news of the Chinese practice of using fishing cormorants, controlled by lines, with rings round their necks to prevent them swallowing the fish?

It is at any rate clear that fish-poaching was a serious hazard for the proprietor of stews or streams. It seems to have been a special ecclesiastical temptation: a wood-cut shows a nun setting a net across a waterfall, and watched by an interested Devil.

CHAPTER 5

'Incorps'd and demi-natur'd'

I

We should probably agree that of all the archetypal images drawn from the natural world, and those to whom we have attached meanings or myths that go far back into folklore, the horse is, or perhaps was, among the most common and in many ways the most terrible; *is*, because (if we believe our soothsayers the psychiatrists) it is the dominant fear-image; *was*, because most of us have now little intimate knowledge of its ways, and perhaps the fear of it when we do confront it is the greater for that. Next to it, in this category, runs the 'Hound', 'my mother's angry dogs' as the image of guilt, revenge, destructive lust; next, perhaps its cousin the wolf; then (so the memories of poems, plays, myths, rise in our minds) bear, tiger, boar, swine, serpent, kite, hawk, raven, crow; swan and dove and heron. I suppose that on general grounds we should expect the Horse and the Rider to be in some way numinous, something which arouses awe: the chariots and horses of the Philistines (so that the light-armed infantry lifted their eyes unto the hills, from whence came their help); the great hymn to the war-horse in the *Book of Job*:

> Did you give the horse his strength?
> Did you clothe his neck with a mane?
> Do you make him quiver like a locust's wings,
> when his shrill neighing strikes terror? . . .
>
> Trembling with eagerness, he devours the ground
> and cannot be held in when he hears the horn;
> at the blast of the horn he cries 'Aha!'
> and from afar he scents the battle.[1]

[1] 39:19ff.

'INCORPS'D AND DEMI-NATUR'D'

I have taken this deliberately from the New English Bible of 1970, for the sake of the new simile 'quiver like a locust's wings', though at some cost to the familiar Authorized Version, 'He saith among the trumpets, Ha, Ha'. Anyone who has ridden to hounds will be familiar with the horse's shivering excitement while waiting outside a covert, his instant response to the hounds breaking and the horn of the mimic warfare. It is unlikely that cavalry will be used again in war, but the instant response of horses to the various bugle-calls is common knowledge.

Of the nightmare horse we have an archetype in Fuseli's terrible painting *The Nightmare*, the great luminous head, the staring eyeballs, that towers above the fainting woman on the bed; recalling the real oppression, the weight on the chest, of that dream; and perhaps the jingle from *King Lear*:

> Swithold footed thrice the wold:
> A' met the nightmare and her nine fold.[1]

which Housman picked up and adapted into a not quite successful image –

> ... Spectres and fears, the nightmare and her foal,
> Drown in the golden deluge of the morn.

So, too, Falstaff's bawdy innuendo:

> I will ride thee o'nights like the mare.[2]

But does not Freud tell us that the *mare* (perhaps Robert Graves' triple-headed goddess) is the cloak for our subliminal Mother-image, that we both revere and dread?

II

Yet there is one fear-image of the horse, perhaps the most terrible and the most complex in all the plays. It is Macbeth's, as his conscience

---

[1] III.4.117. Muir (Arden) points out that night-mare or night more is an incubus, a 'demon', from O.E. *mare*. I am not clear whether Shakespeare knew this.
[2] *2 Henry IV* II.1.78.

twists and writhes before the murder; dreading the supernatural vengeance that will follow the crime. Let us quote the whole passage:

> Besides, this Duncan
> Hath borne his faculties so meek, hath been
> So clear in his great office, that his virtues
> Will plead like angels trumpet-tongu'd against
> The deep damnation of his taking-off;
> And pity, like a naked new-born babe,
> Striding the blast, or heaven's cherubin, hors'd
> Upon the sightless couriers of the air,
> Shall blow the horrid deed in every eye,
> That tears shall drown the wind.[1]

Of all poets and writers who have marvelled at this *terribilità*, Blake came nearest to understanding it. But Blake put in something that is not in Shakespeare; the dead or dying woman (for there are two versions of the drawing) and the babe snatched up from her to 'heaven's cherubin'. The horses he saw as white, and blind, against a background of storm-clouds and rain. We think of his own *Death on the White Horse*; of the white horses of Ibsen's *Rosmersholm*; of the Four Riders of *Revelation*, perhaps as Dürer saw them; the mysterious horses of *Zechariah*, Wagner's *Ride of the Valkyries* and the Choosers of the Slain; perhaps of the fiery horses and riders that pass at night between the two haunted mountains in Sligo, over Yeats's grave: whence (in part at least) the injunction of the Epitaph:

> Horseman, pass by!

So the blind horses of the storm mingle in folk-memory and nightmare with the Wild Hunt; geese baying across a moonlit sky, the phantom riders of many literatures and myths, the huntsman who is Death.

But this passage may also offer a peculiar problem regarding our response to poetry: to which we must bring always our own stored memories and experiences, and particularly those of youth. We may use these consciously in order to recreate the Elizabethan world that provided so many metaphors for poetry, and which is for me, in part,

[1] I.7.16.

'INCORPS'D AND DEMI-NATUR'D'

vécu. We may, in fact piece out our own imperfections of response by trying to discover, imaginatively, the subtleties of the poet's meaning. And it is clear that, as we respond to poetry that is predominantly sensuous, we bring to its realization something of what we ourselves have seen or felt in the past. But it may happen that a wholly extraneous experience may impinge upon us to provide a private interpretation and response.

So with the *Macbeth* passage. A friend and pupil, a distinguished pilot of the second war, had flown on a number of missions of destruction over Germany; and each one filled him with a sense of pity and horror. In relation to these lines, the *office* was R.A.F. slang for the pilot's cockpit, *clear* with its sides and roof of perspex. *Angels* suggested *engines*, the roar of them revved up to the *taking-off*, and its damnation. The bombers strode the rain and the blast; and perhaps far above them moved the angel of pity, for the 'horrid deed'.

III

The 'sightless couriers of the air' do not, I think, owe anything to Shakespeare's own experience. We have the legend, of course, that Shakespeare held horses for a living in London, and when a legend seems quite pointless (as this one is) we must hesitate before we dismiss it. I must confess that Shakespeare's imagery from horsemanship and horses seems, in comparison with that from hawking and hunting, a little distanced, seen from the outside; rather, in fact, like his alleged knowledge of soldiering. Perhaps it is not going too far to say that it is the knowledge of the groom rather than of the rider.

In the first place there are several quite gratuitous pieces of 'horse' description thrown in, which, so far as I can see, do nothing to further the dramatic or narrated action. One is the famous 'points' catalogue of Adonis' horse, cribbed almost word for word from Sylvester's translation of du Bartas. It is true that the horse's pursuit of a fortuitous jennet provides that supreme opportunist Venus with a chance for a discourse on the delights of love, uninhibited and permissive; but I cannot feel that it is really in place. Adonis' horse, indeed, reminds me of Stubbs' eighteenth century paintings:

THE LIVING IMAGE

> Round-hoofed, short-jointed, fetlocks shag and long.
> Broad breast, full eye, small head and nostril wide,
> High crest, short ears, straight leg and passing strong.
> Thin mane, thick tail, broad buttock, tender hide:
> Look, what a horse should have he did not lack . . .[1]

The second extraordinary catalogue is in *The Taming of the Shrew*. It has been pointed out that when Shakespeare re-wrote his source-play he peppered it with allusions from hawking, hunting and horsemanship: but the description of the diseases of the horse that Petruchio in his 'mad humour' chooses to ride is, to say the least, eccentric:

> . . . his horse hipped with an old mothy saddle and stirrups of no kindred; besides, possessed with the glanders and like to mose in the chine; troubled with the lampass, infected with the fashions, full of windgalls, sped with spavins, rayed with the yellows, past cure of the fives, stark spoiled with the staggers, begnawn with the bots, swayed in the back, and shoulder-shotten; near-legged before, and with a half-checked bit, and a head-stall of sheep's leather, which, being restrained to keep him from stumbling, hath been often burst and now repaired with knots; one girth six times pieced, and a woman's crupper of velure, which hath two letters for her name fairly set down in studs, and here and there pieced with packthread.[2]

Now the character who speaks this is Biondello, servant to Lucentio, and quite possibly an ex-groom. We may imagine it delivered as a sort of tour-de-force, a torrent of words, largely alliterated in the Euphuistic manner, like one of those exuberant catalogues in Rabelais, or in Burton's *Anatomy of Melancholy*. But the interesting points are these: there is no original from which Shakespeare wrote this (as he took from Sylvester for *Venus and Adonis*,) and while we can imagine it getting its laugh in the mouth of the servant-clown, (but wholly 'dead' today) it is, as Madden has pointed out,[3] in part the *slang* of horse-diseases; *mosing* should be *mourning*, *fashions* is *farcin*, the *fives* is *vives* – 'certain kernels growing under the horse's ears . . . The Italians call them *vivole*'.

There is therefore something to suggest that Shakespeare himself knew his horses from the point of view of the groom, ostler, farrier,

[1] l.293ff.
[2] III.2.49.
[3] Madden, *op. cit.*, p. 304ff.

'INCORPS'D AND DEMI-NATUR'D'

rather than that of the accomplished horseman. When Falstaff asks 'Where's Bardolph?' we have this:

Page. He's gone into Smithfield to buy your worship a horse.
Falstaff. I brought him in Paul's, and he'll buy me a horse in Smithfield: an I could get me but a wife in the stews, I were manned, horsed, and wived.[1]

Falstaff was no horseman, or he would never have sent another to buy a horse for him.

For horse-coping then, as now, in all countries was notorious for its roguery, and there is a very strange echo of it, often misunderstood, in *Antony and Cleopatra*. We have this piece of dialogue:

Enobarbus (aside to Agrippa). Will Caesar weep?
Agrippa (aside to Enobarbus). He has a cloud in's face.
Enobarbus (aside to Agrippa). He were the worse for that were he a horse; So is he, being a man.[2]

The general sense is obvious: Caesar is depressed, upset, at the parting from his sister Octavia; perhaps in a bad temper. Now, just as we tend to mistrust a black horse (as being sulky) or a very light-coloured bay (as being unreliable in temper) the Elizabethan horse-fancier liked a horse with a white star or blaze on his forehead. 'The horse that hath no white at all upon him is dogged, furious, full of mischief and misfortune'.[3] Such a horse was said to have a 'cloud'. 'Equus nebula (ut vulgo dicitur) in facie, cujus vultus est et melancholicus, jure vituperatur.'[4]

But the horse-coper selling a horse could easily paint a white star or 'blaze' when he was selling a horse; much as cattle dealers in Ireland have been known to disguise the ear-markings of bullocks with clippings from felt-hats, inserted and glued into the punched ear-marks, and covered with glued-on hair. This is an instance where, though the general sense is clear, the detailed implications are not. I have followed Madden's explanation.

[1] *2 Henry IV* 1.2.49.
[2] III.2.51.
[3] Gervase Markham.
[4] Sadleirus, *De procrandis* etc. *equis* (1587), Cit. Madden p. 256.

THE LIVING IMAGE

A good deal of the horse-imagery seems to me tedious and formal; even if we make every possible allowance for our own ignorance, they are so often stereotyped and what Yeats calls 'abstract'. As examples there is the moralizing distich from *Henry V*:

> What rein can hold licentious wickedness
> When down the hill he holds his fierce career?[1]

or from *2 Henry IV*:

> Contention, like a horse
> Full of high feeding, madly hath broke loose
> And bears down all before him.[2]

Behind both we may see the verse of *Jeremiah*:

> They were as fed horses in the morning: every one neighed after his neighbour's wife.[3]

There are the usual baroque allusions: Phaethon and the Horses of the Sun, those fiery-footed steeds of Juliet, and Pegasus the winged horse. Shakespeare does not make much use of the centaur, the noblest of the 'compound' images, except as a type of lust: though the Centaur as an inn figures prominently in *The Comedy of Errors*. The Dauphin in *Henry V* showers classical praises on his horse (Pegasus and Perseus are included in the catalogue) but this is merely to demonstrate Gallic exuberance, deflated by Orleans. One image is good: 'He bounds from the earth as if his entrails were hairs.'[4]

IV

Technical terminology does enter in, and sometimes it is spontaneous. There is the *pacing* in the early stages of training. Horses are to be taught to amble by means of the trammel, off and near legs linked together; so

---
[1] III.3.23; though 'career' (*v. infra*) is also a technical term.
[2] I.I.9.
[3] 5:8. Compare the passage in the Geneva Bible, which was Shakespeare's: 'They rose up in ye morning like fed horses.'
[4] III.7.12.

'INCORPS'D AND DEMI-NATUR'D'

that there is perhaps an ambiguity in the well-known image from *Macbeth*:

> If the assassination
> Could trammel up the consequence, and catch
> With his surcease, success.[1]

with the implications of the outcome being smothered like an active animal in a clinging net, as well as hobbled in its stride. The false gallop or artificial canter was called the *successatura*. The doggerel that Touchstone invents to cap the rhymes found by Rosalind at once suggest this: not only because of the jogging metre, but because the recurrent rhymes on 'Rosalind' suggest the rocking horse motion of hooves striking the ground on either side of the animal, not alternately.[2]

Yet through the pages of Shakespeare there move certain individual horses of nobility and power. Chief among them is Roan Barbary of *Richard II*, the horse that accepted so proudly and willingly the usurper Bolingbroke. The whole passage is worth quoting:

> Groom. O! how it yearn'd my heart when I beheld
> In London streets, that coronation day
> When Bolingbroke rode on roan Barbary,
> That horse that thou so often hast bestrid,
> That horse that I so carefully have dress'd.
>
> K. Rich. Rode he on Barbary? Tell me, gentle friend,
> How went he under him?
>
> Groom. So proudly as if he disdain'd the ground.
>
> K. Rich. So proud that Bolingbroke was on his back!
> That jade hath eat bread from my royal hand;
> This hand hath made him proud with clapping him.

[1] I.7.4. The trammel of today is a fishing net, in which a large-meshed wall of netting is set vertically with floats and leads. On either side are hung loose walls of much finer netting. The fish push this through the larger meshes, and are caught in a sort of purse of their own making. Muir (Arden) explains 'trammel' as a net for partridges: or alternatively a device for hanging pots over a fire. The sense (to me) is that of smothering. *Surcease* is legal. For a root image in tragedy, *v*. Henn, *The Harvest of Tragedy* 2nd ed. London, 1966, Ch. 4.

[2] *As You Like It* III.2.113.

> Would he not stumble? Would he not fall down, –
> Since pride must have a fall, – and break the neck
> Of that proud man that did usurp his back?
> Forgiveness, horse! why do I rail on thee,
> Since thou, created to be aw'd by man,
> Wast born to bear?[1]

Granted that Richard's supreme failure is that of self-pity, granted that he inevitably dramatizes every situation, there is yet a thought for us here. We do ourselves and others much harm in trying to anthropomorphize our animals, in attributing to them human characteristics. Hardy's poem about the pet dog, 'Who is that digging on my grave? is a useful antidote is this kind of sentimentality. In our vanity and weakness we tend to attribute purely human emotions and qualities, such as memory and loyalty, to animals. But that is wrong, It is a shock – I have known it – to return after absence in war and find that one's dog and horse have forgotten one. At first one is inclined to be angry at 'ingratitude'. But King Richard says

> Forgiveness, horse!

And it is worth while to remember the Scots Ballad of *The Twa Corbies*, and the dead knight alone in the heather:

> His hound is to the hunting gane,
>   His hawk to fetch the wildfowl hame;
>   His lady's ta'en anither make –
> So we may mak our dinner sweet.

Then there is the curtal – the outsize trotting horse, what we should now call a heavyweight hunter – that Lafeu rode:

> I'd give bay Curtal, and his furniture,
> My mouth no more were broken than these boys'
> And writ as little beard.[2]

---

[1] v.5.76. 'Barbary' is the generic name for the 'Barb' horse, often crossed with an English mare. The true Arabian blood was first imported into England in the year of Shakespeare's death. (Madden, *op. cit.*, p. 259).
[2] *All's Well* II.3.62. Both 'Curtal' and 'Cut' are, besides being remembered as individual beasts, *any* horses with docked tails.

'INCORPS'D AND DEMI-NATUR'D'

There is the 'poor jade' called 'Cut', whose withers are wrung, galled, hence the *Hamlet* image:

> Let the galled jade wince, our withers are unwrung.[1]

So that in the Carrier's scene (*1 Henry IV* II.1) we get:

> I prithee, Tom, beat Cut's saddle (to even out the lumps), put a few flocks (padding, *sc.* flock mattress) in the point.

V

The technique of training the horse for war was long and complicated. The comprehensive word for it was the 'menage'. There are many images throughout *Hamlet*. The Norman Lamord, who was said by King Claudius to be 'incorps'd and demi-natur'd', was outstanding among the French, who were famed throughout Europe for their horsemanship. 'He grew into his seat'; and the 'shapes and tricks' which he achieved were not mere circus-work. Complete control was essential in the hazards of battle; or even in a duel on horseback – there is a record of one – with wheel-lock pistols. Where weapons are involved much reliance must be placed on the pressure of the knee and thigh. The horse must first be 'paced', to obey the bridle 'to a fine and commendable pace'. Often the image is used in such a way that, while we perceive the general sense, the details may be missed: as when the Duke says to Isabella:

> If you can, pace your wisdom
> In that good path that I would wish it go . . .[2]

which is rather more than his remark a few lines earlier:

> – Show your wisdom, daughter
> In your close patience.[3]

because of the sense of disciplined control. Antony tells Caesar:

---

[1] III.2.243.
[2] *Measure for Measure* IV.3.135.
[3] *Ibid.* 4.3.120.

> The third o' the world is yours, which with a snaffle
> You may pace easy, but not such a wife.[1]

It is in the nature of things that the idea of wifehood should be linked to this, as Hermione's

> Our praises are our wages; you may ride 's
> With one soft kiss a thousand furlongs, ere
> With spur we heat an acre.[2]

The horse must first learn to *pace*: then he must learn the *stop*, which produces Lysimachus' characteristic pun on Quince's unpunctuated prologue to the rude mechanicals' play:

> He hath rid his prologue like a rough colt; he knows not the stop.[3]

A third skill was a strange one: the horse was taught to 'yerk', that is to kick with intent at an enemy, not merely bucking:

> and their wounded steeds
> Fret fetlock-deep in gore, and with wild rage
> Yerk out their armed heels at their dead masters,
> Killing them twice.[4]

A horse will normally do everything to avoid stepping on a recumbent human being; but a war-horse maddened by arrow-wounds would be wholly out of control.

Next, the horse had to be taught to make single and double turns, to 'turn and wind'. He had to learn the 'stop', the violent reining back which threw a horse back on its haunches; a 'career' at full gallop was terminated thus. Both 'career' and 'stop' were essential in the tournament, and this is the meaning of the pun used by Benedick:

> Sir, I shall meet your wit in the career, an you charge it against me.[5]

the metaphor being appropriate to the clash of wits. There is an even clearer statement in *Love's Labour's Lost* of the jousting image:

---

[1] *Antony and Cleopatra* II.2.67.
[2] *Winter's Tale* I.2.91.
[3] *A Midsummer Night's Dream* V.1.118.
[4] *Henry V* IV.7.79.
[5] *Much Ado* V.1.134.

'INCORPS'D AND DEMI-NATUR'D'

> *Boyet.* Full merrily,
> Hath this brave manage, this career, been run.
>
> *Berowne.* Lo, he is tilting straight! Peace! I have done.[1]

Tilting and jousting, with its stylized motions, is a fair image for the contests of witty repartee.

VI

Yet I confess that a survey of Shakespeare's horses leaves me with a profound sense of pity, and of thankfulness for the passing of the horse-drawn economy (I have known it) with its animal suffering. They are subject to every imaginable disease, most of which are caused by ill feeding, as the carriers' scene in *1 Henry IV* makes plain.[2] Peas and beans in the inn-stalls might be 'as dank as a dog', and unscrupulous grooms might butter the horses' hay; knowing that no horse will touch any fodder that has a suspicion of grease on it. Again and again the weary horses are described as 'jades', and they are certainly not pampered. There is little sympathy between the horse and his rider, except when the tiredness of each communicates itself between man and beast, or when a royal horse is pictured in the imagination – like Richard's – as proud of his burden. Shakespeare's horses are whipped, galled, their withers are wrung; they are saddle-sore, they are torn from the 'hot and bloody spur' as the messengers ride over the country about their business, 'the undetermined differences of kings'. Behind them are the ailing horses of the inn-yard at Rochester, the patient shaft-horses, like Dobbin the thill-horse of *The Merchant of Venice*. They are 'sur-reined', driven beyond endurance. They hang their heads, resting before Agincourt:

> In their pale dull mouths the gimmal bit
> Lies foul with chew'd grass, still and motionless.[3]

---

[1] v.2.483.
[2] II.I.I.
[3] *Henry V* IV.2.49. The 'Gimmal bit' was in two pieces, a form of snaffle, linked by a ring. Both men and horses ate grass roots before the battle.

In the background, as in some tapestry of hunting scene, we have the noble horses, fiery, richly-caparisoned, versed in the high school of horsemanship; the perfection of Adonis' horse; Roan Barbary with the Arab head; the nameless paragon of the Dauphin's horse. But my mind goes out to the weary horses I have known and ridden; and to those imagined horses in the arrow-battle, screaming and plunging in pain and fear.

CHAPTER 6

A Review of Bowmen

I

We have seen that a number of bowmen were recruited among the 'shot' of a company as late as 1586, and we know from Ascham the approval and encouragement given to archery as a national sport. From Crecy and Agincourt onwards there had been a battle of weaponry, not unlike that between the tank and the anti-tank gun in the second war, between the armour-piercing arrow as developed by the English bowmen and the plate- or chain-armour of the knights and men-at-arms which was designed to afford a measure of protection against it. In the earlier stage of musket and caliver, military writers suggest that armour should be bullet-proof at ranges of 200–240 yards.[1] And while the theoretical range of the arrow was about the same, its capacity to penetrate chain-mail was not more than a third of this. What kept the bow in use for such a relatively long time was its rapid rate of fire, its cheapness, and its independence of weather; the latter, as well as the erratic behaviour of the powder and the cumbrous miscellaneous equipment was a severe limitation on the matchlock in any form.

The bow had other advantages. It was the property of the individual; it had been whittled and seasoned and shaped to his own needs and ideas. In wet weather it could be carried – as today – in a waxed canvas bow-case: which Shakespeare uses as a term of abuse for a long thin limp person.[2] It could be drawn, aimed and shot once every five or six seconds. Its ammunition was cheap and light, and, in battle, was brought up in the rear of the archery ranks in miniature trucks or handcarts. And although these were 'standard' arrows, and, as government

[1] Webb, *op. cit.* p. 91. Estimates of arrow-penetration varied: one figure given is four inches of oak, but this would be at close range.
[2] *1 Henry IV* II.4.249.

stores, often suspect in quality, they were sufficient to thicken the arrow hail at a range of three-score paces.

The crossbow was a somewhat ambivalent weapon. Its range was half as much again as the long-bow, some three hundred yards. Like other weapon innovations it was held to be un-Christian: the Lateran Council of 1192 had prohibted its use in warfare except against infidels. The experts in its use were mainly mercenaries from Genoa. Purely as a weapon it was of immense power, particularly in its military form. It was cocked either by a compound lever or by a detachable ratchet and brace which drew back the string over the groove in which the arrow or quarrel lay. This was retained in position by a catch, released by compressing a trigger below the 'lock' of the weapon. It had the advantage that, given someone to cock it, it could be released by a child or a woman: whereas the long-bow required a pull of sixty pounds or more, and called for highly-developed muscles in the back and shoulder. For these reasons the Princess in *Love's Labour's Lost*, standing at a 'tryst' to shoot at deer driven past her, would have used a cross-bow. The result was an atrocious alliterated pun:

The preyful princess pierc'd and prick'd a pretty pleasing pricket.[1]

The stone-bow, for which Sir Toby Belch calls in exasperation as the conspirators of *Twelfth Night* watch Malvolio's antics

O! for a stone-bow, to hit him in the eye![2]

is a weapon of some interest, which is only mentioned on this particular occasion. It was a modification of the military crossbow for sporting purposes, and fired a pebble from a pocket or pouch of interlaced string, called the *cradle*. It appeared about 1500, and became popular for killing game birds on the ground by day, or, with the aid of a lantern, knocking roosting birds out of trees at night. Later the air-gun or the smaller bore rifle was used for the same purpose, particularly by poachers at night for taking roosting pheasants. All such birds present a large target at night, especially in leafless trees.

---

[1] *Love's Labour's Lost* IV.2.57. 'Pricket = second year; 'spayed', third; stag, fourth; fifth, 'great stag'; sixth, a hart. (*Boke of St. Albans*, III.)
[2] II.5.46.

A REVIEW OF BOWMEN

It is possible, though I do not know of a reference, that the pebble was sometimes replaced by a number of smaller stones loosely tied up in a piece of cloth; much as a catapult might be used today with small shot done up in tissue paper, instead of the single buckshot familiar to the schoolboy.

The stone-bow, being an aristocratic arm, was often elaborately decorated. The stock usually terminated in a ball which was held under the arm-pit. As a short range weapon of precision it was often equipped with front and rear sights to guide the missile. Alternative names are *prodd, latch,* or *arbalete à jalet*.[1] But the crossbow had three enormous disadvantages. In its most powerful forms it was slow to cock and load. Its ammunition was so heavy that, though the official issue for battle was fifty 'quarrels' or bolts per man, it was impossible for the individual soldier to carry more than eighteen. Above all, the lateral space required to shoot the crossbow was considerable, especially if accidents were to be avoided. The ranks were thus inevitably opened out, and to that extent more vulnerable to cavalry and to opposing infantry with swords and pikes. With the long-bow they could stand almost shoulder to shoulder, as riflemen were to do later. Sometimes attempts were made to combine the cross-bow with a gunpowder weapon.

II

We may now turn to the exegesis of two classic passages in Shakespeare. King Lear in madness is enlisting, and reviewing his troops; jousting, hawking; watching practice at the archery butts:

> . . . There's your press-money. That fellow handles his bow like a crow-keeper: draw me a clothier's yard. Look! Look! a mouse. Peace, peace! this piece of toasted cheese will do't. There's my gauntlet; I'll prove it on a giant. Bring up the brown bills. O! well flown, bird: i' the clout, i' the clout.[2]

For the second passage:

---

[1] See in general Sir Ralph Payne-Galway, *The Crossbow*. There are some beautifully decorated examples in The Wallace Collection.
[2] IV.6.86.

THE LIVING IMAGE

Jesu! Jesu! dead! a' drew a good bow; and dead! a' shot a fine shoot: John a Gaunt betted much money on his head. Dead! a' would have clapped i' the clout at twelve score; and carried you a forehand shaft a fourteen and fourteen and a half, that it would have done a man's heart good to see. How a score of ewes now?[1]

It is difficult to see just why these speeches of Shallow and Silence should be so moving. Perhaps it is their rich irrelevancy as in Shallow's last sentence: more, perhaps, the plangency of the rhythm, an accent which Synge caught: we may think perhaps of the impression given of Patch Darcy in *In the Shadow of the Glen*, and of the decay of all strengths and skills.

We may take the passages line by line. Lear's 'press money' is of course Elizabethan. The scene is detailed in Falstaff's recruiting of his 'ragamuffins', the 'food for powder'. The Commissioners for the Press issued warrants to the Chief Constables of Hundreds, who in their turn issued warrants to the Petty Constables of towns and hamlets. These produced before the Commissioners 'so many able and sufficient men as they were charged with in their warrants'. From these men the Commissioners chose, by 'pricking', the men they required. These were given twelve pence (the Queen's Shilling of Hardy and Housman) and by accepting it were legally enlisted. They were then put in charge of the draft-conducting officer 'together with eight pence a day for their charges'. Both on that progress, and subsequently, every kind of corruption was practised. As an example, each commander expected to include in his pay, as a perquisite, that of soldiers who had died or deserted, or even who had never existed. These were known as 'dead pays'.

Lear's imagination is first caught by a clumsy member of the draft. The use of boys or country youths to keep birds off crops or fruit was common. I have known it done by such with blank charges of black powder in ancient guns.[2] The 'crowkeeper', scaring rooks or such like off fruit or corn, would squat down clumsily: Ascham notes this. Only

---

[1] *2 Henry IV* III.2.47.
[2] The modern method consists of lengths of slow-burning fuse, set with explosive charges at intervals.

an archer of exceptional physique would be able to draw an arrow of a 'clothier's yard';[1] that picturesque arrow of romantic tales was too long for accurate shooting, and would in any case have involved drawing to the ear instead of the later method of drawing to the jaw. The standard arrow at Agincourt was twenty-nine inches long including the head, and weighed seven silver shillings. The 'brown bills' were weapons somewhat shorter than the pike; its head being a hooked blade with projecting spikes of various patterns and painted to prevent rust. Webb[2] quotes Sir Roger Williams as complaining of their quality of temper; the common brown bills are 'lightly for the most part all iron with a little steel or none at all'. He proposed a proportion of only 200 billmen to every thousand pikemen. We may suppose that Lear imagines a special small squad of the 'brown bills'; they would require more training of rustic recruits than the relatively simple pike, for their drill motions were more complicated.

The image-clusters in Lear's mind move naturally, with the exception of the mouse and the toasted cheese. The last but one is applause for a brilliant stoop by a hawk; the last of all (perhaps the link is the thud of the falling bird and the thud of the arrow in the mark or clout) brings us back to archery exercise. The 'clout' was the square piece of canvas, the target for the butts; the white mark on it was known as the 'prick'. Ranges were estimated in scores of paces. Twelve score or 240 yards was the extreme range, though the 'distance' feat of Shallow's friend of 280 to 290 yards would have been free flight with a considerable elevation. The 'forehand shaft', according to *Toxophilus*, was the aimed shot, contrasted with the 'shot of adventure', the arrow loosed at random into the 'brown' of the enemy. The classic instance is at *1 Kings* 22:34: 'And a certain man drew a bow at a venture, and smote the King of Israel between the joints of the harness.' The throat and the armpits were particularly vulnerable points. The longest recorded distance is 972 yards 2¾ inches, said to have been made by Sultan Selim II of

---

[1] Now, the normal 36″: but by a Statute of Edward VI, 'Cloth was to be meten and measured by the yarf, adding to every yard one inch by the rule'. cf. the 'poulter's measure', 12 plus 14, for alternate dozens of eggs; and the unpleasant Elizabethan metre of that name.

[2] Webb, *op. cit.* p. 91.

Turkey. The modern record is 937·13 yards made in America in 1959; the British record is just over 500 yards.[1] For comparison, 'long range' rifle competitions at Bisley are shot at 900 and 1000 yards.

But far more important than the extreme ranging power, and the mythical feats of accuracy at those distances in the Robin Hood type of story, was the extreme rapidity of aimed fire – ten to twelve shots a minute, for the archer in battle order has his arrows stuck in a semi-circle into the ground immediately in front of him – and the almost incredible penetrative power of the arrows of Agincourt and their modern counterparts. In a recent experiment a lay figure was dressed in fifteenth century chain armour: an arrow passed clean through the armour and the figure, and bulged out the mail on the far side. A modern game-hunting arrow will penetrate a five-gallon steel drum filled with sand. A certain amount of hunting of dangerous game as well as deer is still done with this weapon, in Africa and North America. As I write a controversy is raging among bow-hunters in America, for whom the deer season is extended substantially beyond that for firearms, as to whether it is sporting to use collars soaked with anaesthetic drugs at the base of the arrow-heads. Anaesthetic darts are of course familiar to big-game conservationists.

The war-bow as developed after Crecy and Agincourt was of Spanish or Mediterranean yew, the rough staves being brought in bundles as deck-cargo on ships bringing the wine of the country to English ports. So William Morris, of Chaucer's Thames-bank –

> Think that below bridge the green lapping waves
> Smite some few keels that bear Levantine staves
> Cut from the yew wood on the burnt-up hill,
> And pointed jars that Greek hands toiled to fill . . .
> While nigh the throng'd wharf Geoffrey Chaucer's pen
> Moves over bills of lading.

The soldier himself bought his bow-stave; shaped, seasoned and waxed it to his liking. Ascham gives elaborate directions for shaping and waxing the bow, and its general care and maintenance. The price of the raw bow-staves rose by a factor of six during the reign of Elizabeth. Its length would vary between five feet and something over six feet, ac-

---

[1] From P. A. W. Warner, *Sieges of the Middle Ages*.

cording to the taste and physique of the archer. The longer the bow the less likely it was to break in battle. For hunting purposes a shorter and handier weapon of about five feet was preferred. Its pull varied between fifty and seventy-five pounds: the muscular effort may be imagined if we think of lifting a seventy-five pound weight on a thin string hooked round the second joints of the first three fingers. It is often supposed that the arrow itself is drawn. This is not so: the fingers of the right hand are hooked round the bow-string with the arrow supported between them. Only thus is it possible to get the correct 'loose' on which accuracy depends.

Modern bows are sometimes made of steel, but more commonly of laminated wood and fibre-glass. The pull is suited to the individual, from forty to seventy pounds. The length varies from sixty to seventy-two inches. The arrows, usually of cedar, aluminium or fibre-glass, are matched as regards their 'spine' or stiffness to the 'cast' of the bow. Their length varies from twenty-seven to twenty-nine inches.

Twice Shakespeare mentions another kind of bow, the Tartar's, but apparently as a weapon that had acquired some reputation in the long warfares of the Middle East. This was a very short stiff bow, composite, of horn and sinew, and shaped in such a way as to give what is still known as 'the Turkish recurve'; the limbs being adjusted so that the full power of their extremities does not come into play until the bow is strung and partly drawn. With this weapon extraordinarily long shots, using the small light arrows known as 'sipers', were possible. It was well-adapted for cavalry work with highly-skilled horsemen who could ride without touching the briddle-reins. Hence Puck's simile

–I go
Swifter than arrow from the Tartar's bow.[1]

and the derisory comment:

We'll have no Cupid hood-wink'd with a scarf,
Bearing a Tartar's bow of lath,
Scaring the ladies like a crow-keeper.[2]

[1] *A Midsummer Night's Dream* III.2.101.
[2] *Romeo and Juliet* 1.4.3. *cf.* the 'dagger of lath' of the song in *Twelfth Night*.

Cupid's bow is constantly represented in iconography in this form; the shape being associated with the curves of mouth and lips. And it must be short, in view of Cupid's own height, to be manageable.

III

Shakespeare very wisely does not attempt any description of the arrow battles either at the Siege of Harfleur or at Agincourt. There are merely the trumpet-calls, 'alarums and excursions', in the background. The best account I know of this last is imaginary, but it is amply documented, was written by a practising archer, and seems to me what Aristotle would call 'a more philosophical and a higher thing than history'.[1] The characters involve an archer called John Bates, and the Officer Commanding Archers, Sir Thomas Erpingham:

> Bates' Company was in the centre of the English line. That line was a thousand yards long by six men deep, composed of one thousand knights and men-at-arms and five thousand archers. In battle one's eyes see only what is close in front of them. Bates in the centre saw only that menacing line of iron rolling towards him. He was vaguely aware of men shouting on both flanks and of horses screaming. He saw a riderless charger madly gallop across his front, to fall in a kicking heap, bristling with arrows. That was precisely the fate that had befallen the French cavalry which charged the English flanks. Two thousand horsemen had charged in, within five hundred paces of Bates, but such is the fog of fighting that all he had noticed was one riderless horse . . .

The archers hold their fire until the line of French knights is fifty or sixty yards away:

> There arose an indescribable and awful sound – the sound of a thousand bows twanging and a thousand arrows whistling simultaneously through the air; the sound of a hurricane lashing at a forest; the sound of a thousand steel arrow-heads hurtling against a wall of casques and breastplates with the din of an insane boiler-works and hundreds of furious pneumatic riveters and ber-

---

[1] 'Weston Martyr', *Bowmen's Battle. Blackwood's Magazine* August 1938. No. 1474. Several historians have confirmed to me the general authenticity of this impressive story, and I am glad to be able to pay a humble tribute to it.

serk drilling machines roaring in raging haste. Each shaft that struck square struck down; if it did not penetrate and kill, it felled its man with a blow as from a sledgehammer.[1] Each arrow that struck at an angle shattered itself in a shower of sparks, or glanced aside to strike again beyond.

Presently the arrow storm slackened and ceased. Its clanging roar died slowly out, like the passing of tropical hail beating, then tapping, on corrugated iron roofs.

Bates stopped shooting when he looked for a standing man to shoot at and saw nothing but a line of bodies heaped up three deep. He wiped the sweat from his face and stood marvelling. And well he might; for the bare face of the ploughed field that had become a field of battle had grown a crop of arrow shafts as thick as a field of wind-laid wheat.

The writer suggests, and supports his figures, that, in the twenty minutes of the battle, one million arrows were fired at a target 1000 yards long and 10 yards wide: that is, ten arrows per square yard.

There is one famous arrow image, in *Hamlet*. The King says to Laertes, after speaking of the spring at King's Newnham which had the property of ossifying wood,

> . . . so that my arrows
> Too slightly timbered for so loud a wind,
> Would have reverted to my bow again.[2]

Ascham has much to say on the effect of the weather on archery. Frost and damp are deadly enemies of the bow. Temperature and humidity as well as the various kinds of wind must be allowed for. A competent archer must be a 'good weather man',[3] 'like a good shipman'. 'Weake

---

[1] Two confirming instances. An American archery catalogue gives the shocking power of big-game archery equipment as comparable to that of a .50 calibre bullet at 50 yards. 'During a rehearsal of a scene for the film of *Robin Hood*, Mr. Howard Hill, who is a noted American archer, loosed a (blunt) arrow at a mounted man wearing a steel breastplate covered with two inches of balsa wood, and knocked him clean out of the saddle.' 'Weston Martyr', *op. cit.* Even with armour that was supposed to be arrow- or even musket-proof, the impact of the missile would be serious; and it was for such 'inward bruises' that spermaceti was valuable.

[2] IV.7.21.

[3] Ascham, *op. cit.* p. 208.

bowes and light shaftes cannot stande in a rough wind'.[1] The archer must be familiar with the performance of each of his arrows under different conditions. (His full equipment seems to have been forty shafts for general shooting practice.)[2] He notes that 'there is no feather but only of a goose that hath all commodities in it'[3] and he is highly contemptuous of peacock feathers that many men have taken up for 'gaynesse'. He would not have approved of Chaucer's Yeoman, who had, under his belt, 'A sheef of pecok-arwes brighte and kene . . .'

The bow has its own mystique. The most famous in mythology is the bow of Hercules, which he bequeathed at his death to Philoctetes. That drama Edmund Wilson[4] regarded as a type-myth of our civilization; the possessor of power, suffering from the wound which does not heal. The second, perhaps, is the bow of Odysseus, which he found, after so many years, still 'live' on his return. Again the bow is a symbol of supreme power, of skill that has not failed, even in age, whatever the limitations of the body. The contest in archery in the Hall before the suitors have recognized Odysseus is not incredible; nor is that tremendous revenge by the deadly arrows. Perhaps the mystique consists, in part, in that – unlike the gun – the archer still depends on his strength and skill, which cannot be bought; and on his gear which he can make and maintain himself. To those who have not shot with it it is still a term of derision, of obsolete armaments, or a child's toy. Those who have used it are aware of its power and its terror. The arrow that flieth by day is as terrible as the pestilence of the night.[5] They are emblems of many things: of desire, of Diana's moonlight, of revenge, and the power of the battle. Above and behind them is Sagittarius, the Archer of the Constellations, and the lights that underlie his bow; as well as man's emblem and the archer who shoots at a star,[6] and whose arrows, tuned to the proper resonance, may unite to form a bridge to heaven.[7]

[1] *Ibid.* p. 206.
[2] *Ibid.* p. 90.
[3] *Ibid.* p. 171.
[4] *The Wound and the Bow*: London, 1952.
[5] *Psalms* 91:5.
[6] e.g. as in Yeats's 'Parnell's Funeral'.
[7] *The Golden Bough*.

CHAPTER 7

A Note on Shakespeare's Army

> . . . And that it was great pity, so it was,
> This villainous saltpetre should be digg'd
> Out of the bowels of the harmless earth,
> Which many a good tall fellow had destroy'd
> So cowardly; and but for these vile guns
> He would himself have been a soldier.
>
> *1 Henry IV.* 1.3.59
>
> We vainly accuse the fury of guns, and the new inventions of death.
>
> SIR THOMAS BROWNE, *Religio Medici* I

I

It seems to have been one of the fallacies of Shakespearean critics at the turn of the nineteenth century to argue deductively from Shakespeare's apparent experiences backwards to his 'practical' life. His seamanship, it was said, was excellent (it is not in fact outstanding): therefore he might have sailed with Drake on his voyage round the Horn. His law is excellent (it has since been shown that it is not): therefore he must have been Bacon, or, (perhaps) another lawyer. It was not until Croce that this basic fallacy was dispersed; though indeed there was no need to go beyond the Elizabethan critics who had pointed out, of that mass of sonnets in the 1590's, that a man might write of love, and not be in love. There are amusing by-products; as of Shakespeare being praised as a botanist for his anticipation of plant genetics, because of the lines from *A Midsummer Night's Dream*:

> And when she weeps, weeps every little flower
> Lamenting some enforcéd chastity.[1]

– ignoring the fact that *enforcéd* meant, not compulsively chaste, but raped. For the rapid, accurate and even encyclopaedic absorbtion of

[1] III.1.198.

technical knowledge we need go no further than the story of Kipling, and of the young engineer who, after reading 'The Ship that Found Herself', sought leave of his firm to attend the university at which Kipling was Professor of Marine Engineering.

A book of the 'amateur' or 'armchair' layer of criticism founded on the fallacy mentioned above is Duff Cooper's *Sergeant Shakespeare*. Shakespeare could not in any event have been a Sergeant: such a post demanded great experience, and went to men of seniority and 'of much traffic in the wars'. But in fact Shakespeare's knowledge is, as we should expect from that myriad-minded man, no more profound than that which would be gathered by an exceptionally acute and retentive intellect, accustomed to drawing out in talk men of infinitely varied characters, professions, outlook.

There are two important recent works dealing with the subject of Shakespeare's Army: Paul A. Jorgensen's *Shakespeare's Military World*[1] and Henry J. Webb's *Elizabethan Military Science*.[2] Professor Webb is a historian who was attached to the American Army during the Second War. Both books are admirable. My own contribution to the matter of imagery is based on my experience as a soldier, and on some practical experience with some of the types of firearms and explosives which were used in the Elizabethan Army. This aspect of my early education was largely accidental; it was not unlike that of Richard Jefferies in *The Amateur Poacher*.

II

We may glance briefly at the general picture. Shakespeare's army was, apart from its few professionals like Fluellen and Gower, a ramshackle affair. It was raised to meet specific emergencies, such as the threat of the Armada. The method of drafting men was basically erratic and corrupt; Falstaff's assessment of his band of ragamuffins is humorous, but it is not all a parody. The theoretical war-establishments bear little relationship to what was actually put in the field. The arms, like those of the Home Guard in the 1940's, were based on what could be procured

[1] Berkeley and C.U.P., 1956.
[2] Wisconsin and London, 1965.

A NOTE ON SHAKESPEARE'S ARMY

or improvised; hence the emphasis on the pike. Theoretically, a company of 150 to 120 men was divided into 'shot' (firearms and bows), halberdiers and pikemen. Bowmen were still being recruited in 1586, when firearms were becoming general,[1] and there was an attempt to revive the bow as a military weapon as late as 1625. But it should be remembered that it was the armour-piercing arrow, as developed at Creçy and Agincourt, that spelt the destruction of the armoured knight, who had long been forced to seek protection behind an extra shield or 'pavise', carried by some kind of assistant.

An Elizabethan Army drawn up for a set-piece battle presented an interesting picture. On either or both flanks were the guns, well aside from the main body. The centre consisted of both the 'shot' and the pikemen; these last being the most 'honourable', and probably the best drilled. We may quote an example of Tudor prose that sets out their virtues:

> Let the pikeman march with a good grace, holding up his head gallantly, his face full of gravity and state and such as is fit for his person; and let his body be straight and as much upright as possible; and that which is most important is that they have their eyes always upon their companions which are in rank with them and before them, going just one with another, and keeping perfect distance without committing the least error in pace or step. And every pace and motion they ought to make at one instant of time. And in this sort all the ranks ought to go, sometimes softly, sometimes fast, according to the stroke of the drum . . . So shall they go just and even with a gallant and sumptuous pace; for by doing so they shall be esteemed, honoured and commended by all the lookers on, who shall take wonderful delight to behold them.[2]

The reason for this precision is not hard to find. It was the pikeman who was the defence of the whole body of infantry against charging cavalry; kneeling with the butt of his pike on the ground, the point outwards so as to form a *cheveux-de-frise*. If the discipline were not perfect the whole line was vulnerable. Therefore the pikeman (who was also armed with a sword or rapier) was one of the most 'honourable'

---
[1] Webb *op. cit.* p. 85. But one of the great difficulties was maintaining, storing and repairing them.
[2] William Garrard, *The Art of Warre*, 1591.

members of the company. His stance – and courage – was the same as that which had been practised since Homeric times in withstanding the charges of wild beasts[1] notably boars. He had to possess both strength and coolness. To the enemy the lines of pikemen must have seemed formidable. William Morris has put it vividly:

> As clearly as they saw thy townsmen meet
> Those who in vineyards of Poictou withstood
> The glittering horror of the steel-tipped wood.[2]

The pikeman had to be well-disciplined and of powerful physique, for the pike was a massive weapon, between fifteen and twenty feet in length, and strengthened by iron plates. In the 'push of pike' the weapon was supported horizontally by the left hand while the soldier advanced. The bowmen we may think of as trained men, and the practice of archery had long been the only approved sport in England. The phenomenal accuracy attained by the long-bow was the result of training since childhood.

The 'shot', the term used for gunpowder weapons, would be armed either with musket, arquebus, or caliver. Of these Shakespeare mentions the musket only once, with somewhat 'precious' imagery in the mouth of Helena:

> . . . and is it I
> That drive thee from the sportive court, where thou
> Wast shot at with fair eyes, to be the mark
> Of smoky muskets? O you leaden messengers,
> That ride upon the violent speed of fire,
> Fly with false aim . . .[3]

and much else of a somewhat rhetorical nature. We need not wonder at the 'eyes' image: there is an extremely frigid sonnet in *Zepheria* (1594) which refers to the lover and the lady's eyes:

> How have I joyed to wanton in your sight
> Though I was slain by your artillery![4]

[1] Hence the image in *Cymbeline* v.3.8: 'Like lions upon the pikes o' the hunters.'
[2] *The Earthly Paradise*. Velasquez' picture, *The Surrender at Breda*, shows, in the right background, such a forest of pikes.
[3] *All's Well* III.2.104.
[4] *Elizabethan Sonnet-Cycles*, ed. M. F. Crow. London, 1896–8.

A NOTE ON SHAKESPEARE'S ARMY

The musket was immensely heavy and cumbrous: it could only be fired from a rest, and the 'drill' to handle it and its accessories was prolonged and intricate. Its range was a matter of debate among contemporary military authorities. We shall not be far off if we put the effective range at a hundred yards, and the maximum at two hundred. The musket was highly unpopular with the troops because of its weight and its bulky ammunition.[1] The harquebuse or arquebus was the lightest weapon; the caliver, with a 42-inch barrel, intermediate between the arquebus and the musket. The caliver was superseding the other matchlocks by 1596; its consumption of powder was much lighter. The powder required for the musket was one pound for twelve rounds; compared with three drams of black powder or its equivalent bulk in 'smokeless' powder, for a twelve-bore today.

III

It is relevant at this stage to describe the practical handling of these weapons. They were all firelocks: that is to say the powder in the barrel had to be ignited by a slow-match dipping into a pan (with a cover that moved sideways on a pivot) of priming-powder at the touch-hole. The flint-lock, so long the standard weapon of the British Army under the affectionate name of 'Brown Bess', did not come into use till the end of the seventeenth century.

To load it, the stock was placed on the ground and the barrel tilted away from the firer at an angle of about 60°, for at this stage accidents were common. Next, the charge of powder was poured into the barrel from a flask hanging at the soldier's belt. The nozzle of the flask had, later, a lever with two shutters which served as a measure for the quantity of powder as well as providing a safety cut-off to insulate the rest of the contents. Nothing was easier than for a spark from the burning residue to run back through the live powder and to burst in the soldier's hand. Hence –

> Like powder in a skill-less soldier's flask,
> To set a-fire by thine own ignorance.[2]

[1] The barrel was 54 inches long.
[2] *Romeo and Juliet* III.3.131.

But the flask is the source of some fairly complex imagery. Its shape and function inevitably made it, like the pistol (and to some extent all firearms), a phallic image. One of Webster's villains is apprehended in an attempt at assassination with a pistol concealed in his codpiece. Donne uses the image freely:

> Who would not laugh at mee, if I should say
> I saw a flaske of *powder burne a day?*
> ('The Broken Heart')

and in the 'Nocturnall on St. Lucie's Day'

> The Sunne is spent, and now his flasks
> Send forth light squibs, no constant rays.

The 'light squibs' were the changes of powder, without a bullet on top of the charge, used in the training of recruits: to accustom them to the flash from the pan, and without the ferocious recoil from the fully-loaded weapon. They are adequate symbols for the sun as the diminished source of sexual energy at the 'year's midnight'.

When the powder had been poured in, the soldier tapped the barrel, still carefully holding it away from him. Next came wadding in some form or other. Then came the bullet, taken from yet another pouch, or, if the soldier were on sentry-duty, from several held in his mouth. This too would be followed by wadding to keep in the loosely-fitting ball. Each operation required a ram-rod. Traditionally the powder was packed as tightly as possible, the ball or shot only sufficiently to make sure that it was retained in the barrel.

The soldier then turned his attention to the lock. By Shakespeare's time the firelock had reached the limits of its development. Essentially the mechanism consisted of the S-shaped 'cock' or 'serpentine', designed so that the upper portion held the slow-match, or length of string dipped in a solution of saltpetre and alcohol.[1] The 'cock' was held back against a spring by a simple scear and release, actuated by a trigger. The pressure required for the release, as in a modern target-rifle, could be varied by filing out the notch. A very light pressure, firing at a touch, could provide an image for characters who laughed too readily:

[1] I have made this by steeping string in the water in which spinach has been boiled.

A NOTE ON SHAKESPEARE'S ARMY

... make those laugh whose lungs are tickle o' the sere.[1]

But before dealing with his match the soldier had to make sure that the touch-hole, bored through the barrel at right angles to the base of the powder-charge, was open, and he cleared this with a needle or pricker. From yet another flask or box a finer powder was forced through this hole, and a small quantity heaped in a pan beside it. Failure to clear the touch-hole properly could lead to the proverbial flash-in-the-pan, or 'false fire', with which the recruit would be frightened.[2]

Finally the slow-match had to be fitted into the clamp in the serpentine and blown into a glow sufficient to ignite the powder. If firing were delayed it had constantly to be adjusted so that the burning end was always of the right length. It might easily go out: hence he was required to have about his person a long piece of match, lit at both ends; with another spare piece of match, and flint and steel with which to re-kindle it. This, in proximity to the flasks and possibly a bandolier of paper *cartouches*, holding ready-made charges of powder, was a further hazard.

But perhaps worst of all was the problem of the trigger of the matchlock, which originally consisted of a long lever beneath the lock-work, and was at first unprotected by any form of trigger guard. Hence Gervase Markham's complaint:

> Let the cocks and trickers be nimble to goe and come; for as concerning seares they are utterly out of date, and the Inconueniences thereof are found in our daily experience; for upon every motion or touch of the Soldiers garments, they are apt to make the piece fly off, killing sometimes him that marcheth behind, sometimes him that is before; sometimes sets fire to him that beares it, and sometimes wounds his Officer that comes to giue him direction.

But in addition the infantryman had a considerable amount of ancillary equipment. As well as the flasks for powder, his bullet-pouches, and something to contain the wadding, he had a bullet-mould, a pricking needle, and a corkscrew device called a worm for drawing unfired

---

[1] *Hamlet* II.2.328. The modern equivalent is 'hair-triggered'.
[2] *Hamlet* III.2.269: 'What! frighted with false fire?'

charges and for cleaning the barrel.[1] For every ten soldiers there was an iron cauldron for melting lead. He would have rags or tow to use, with the ram-rod, for the long and dirty job of scouring the barrel at intervals during and after firing. All this equipment was in addition to his armour and his sword. In the light of this we may examine the scene during the mustering of recruits. Falstaff points out to Shallow the virtues of the puny and ragged Wart:

> ... a' shall charge you and discharge you with the motion of a pewterer's hammer.[2]

Like the 'brazen canstick' this is a memory of the metal workers' quarter in the City. Bardolph is ordered to put a caliver into Wart's hands. Elementary instruction begins with Wart learning to hold up the weapon, and move it from side to side; its considerable weight provided scope for comic business:

> *Falstaff.* Come, manage me your caliver. So: very well: go to: very good: exceeding good. O, give me always a little, lean, old, chopp'd, bald shot. Well said, i'faith, Wart; thou'rt a good scab: hold, there's a tester for thee.
>
> *Shallow.* (*always a pessimist*) He is not his craft's master, he doth not do it right. I remember at Mile-end Green, when I lay at Clement's Inn – I was then Sir Dagonet in Arthur's show, – there was a little quiver fellow, and a' would manage you his piece thus: and 'would about and about, and come you in, and come you in; 'rah, tah, tah', would a' say; 'bounce', would a' say; and away again would a' go, and again would a' come: I shall never see such a fellow.

The passage is worth comment in some detail. The pikeman and the archer had to be men of powerful physique: the crossbow and the matchlock – always excepting the heavy musket – could be managed be a 'little, lean, old, chopp'd, bald shot'. Here the essential was neatness and speed, for as a drill movement it took fourteen motions to load and eighteen to discharge the piece. Hence the possibility of unlimited confusion among the levies, many of them country labourers,

---

[1] It was not difficult to leave the ramrod in the barrel before firing; a frequent cause of accidents.
[2] *2 King Henry IV* III.2.271.

A NOTE ON SHAKESPEARE'S ARMY

raised in emergency. Shallow's friend at Clement's Inn was what we should call a Territorial; he had learnt his drill on the parade ground at Mile End where the trained bands were exercised. He is a little *quiver* fellow – the image in its ambiguities suggests both energy and resourcefulness, as contrasted with the limp and pejorative 'bowcase'.[1] They would 'about and about', for the organization of the ranks depended on the fact that a trained musketeer could re-load in the time that it took six other men to aim and fire theirs. The file were therefore organised so that

> ... if the Battalia stand, the first Ranke having giuen their vollie shall fall back to the Reare either in wheele or countermarch, and the second Ranke shall come into their places and giue their vollie and so consequently all the rest.[2]

If the procedure seems unduly slow, it should be remembered that the musketeer had, besides reloading, to see to his match, and to position the massive barrel on its rest. Shallow's fellow-student – in a stage production we should remember that Shallow seizes Wart's caliver and 'drills' with it – fires, turns round, urges the next man to take his place in the firing line, and makes encouraging noises while he reloads. 'Bounce' might represent the final impact of the ram-rod as the bullet was driven home; ascertained by dropping the rod 'free' into the barrel, and noting the sound, and the distance of its recoil.[3]

IV

'Villainous Saltpetre'

There is a satirical illustration of an alchemically-minded monk mixing an explosive mixture in his laboratory, closely watched by the devil. Gunpowder was in any event a mysterious substance. To Whitehorne Saltpetre was

> a mixture of manie substances, gotten out with fire and water of drie and durtie grounde, or of that flower, that groweth out of new walles, in cellars,

---

[1] *v.* p. 77 *infra*.
[2] Gervase Markham, *op. cit.*
[3] My own time for reloading a muzzle-loading shot-gun was about one minute per barrel. But then I did not have to manipulate the priming and the match.

or of that grounde which is found loose within toombes, or desolate caues: in which grounde (according to my judgement) the same is engendered by an airy moistness drunke up, and gotten of the yearthie drynes: whose nature (by the effect thereof) considering, I cannot tell how to be resolved, to say what things properly it is.[1]

Many besides Whitehorne were puzzled by this simple mixture of saltpetre, sulphur and charcoal. Its origin is lost in mystery. Friar Bacon first described it in Western Europe. There is no evidence for the myth that it was first discovered by the Chinese, who used it only for making fireworks. The *Book of Fires* attributed to Marcus Graecus was in circulation before 1300, and described both gunpowder and rockets.

From the point of view of the Elizabethan soldier it was a chancy and unsatisfactory substance. Its manufacture appears to have been a trade secret; for as late as 1662, a member of the Royal Society, being deputed to investigate its nature and composition, had to bribe his way into a powder factory.[2] Yet Whitehorne gives directions for making 'Finer and Stronger Handegun Poulder', and there are instructions as to how to test a newly-broached cask by touch, smell and taste. There was even a device like a miniature pistol (which persisted well into the nineteenth century) in which a small quantity of powder could be fired and its strength registered on a scale. The problem of the basically erratic nature of 'government' powder was not solved till the middle of the seventeenth century, 'Corn' powder was made by dissolving the mixture into a slurry and then passing it through sieves.

There was also an officer who had charge of various ancillary troops: the 'trench master', responsible for throwing up earthworks, the mine-master, or the fire-master,[3] though I cannot find any account of these in the regular war establishments. The Elizabethan Army experimented freely with all manner of incendiary and explosive devices. The incendiary 'bullets wrapped in fire'[4] had various recipes, as Whitehorne's

---

[1] Whitehorne. Searchers for saltpetre were 'licensed to dig in dovecotes, barns, stables and outhouses, provided they re-erected any buildings that collapsed as a result of their activities' . . . (Cruickshank, *op. cit.* p. 127.)
[2] Sprat's *The History of the Royal Society* p. 260.
[3] Webb, *op. cit.* p. 125.
[4] *King John* II.1.227.

A NOTE ON SHAKESPEARE'S ARMY

Sarpentin poulder V partes, saltpetre refined IV partes, Rasapina I parte, Camfer haufe a parte, turpentine haufe a parte, haufe a parte of oyle of stones and oyl of lintesed, as much of the one as of the other, Aqua vite hauf a parte.[1]

The mixture was to be made into tow-covered balls. Like napalm of which it is a forerunner, it could not be quenched by water. Nor could the celebrated Greek Fire of which the composition is unknown. Of his own bullets Whitehorne says:

> but if this composition chance to the throwen and lighte upon armour, it will make it glowing redde in such sort, that he that hath it on his backe shalbe constrained to put it off, if he will not be burnt to death.

'Fireworks' of various kind could be attached to thrusting weapons, and this is presumably the source of the allusion in *Henry VIII*:

> That fire-drake did I hit three times on the head, and three times was his nose discharged against me: he stands there, like a mortar-piece, to blow us.[2]

This spirited but slightly obscure passage, describing the 'tumult' in the Palace Yard, is a curious medley. The fire-drake can also mean 'a fire sometimes seen flying in the night like a dragon' which may possibly be picked up by the phrase a few lines further on, 'I missed the meteor once'. The mortar is the large-bore short weapon designed to fire with a high trajectory. The 'file of boys' throwing stones in the melée are described with some humour as 'loose shot'.

V

'And the outrageous cannon'

We frequently speak as if the coming of heavy artillery revolutionized Tudor warfare. This is very far from the truth. The artillery component of the army had no fixed establishment, and the number of guns employed on the battlefields is surprisingly small. Shakespeare speaks generally of cannon, and only once details three of the generally accepted

[1] In his translation of Machiavelli's *The Arte of War*, 1560–62.
[2] v.4.43. There is, of course, as the commentators point out, the pun on the opponent's red nose.

eight groups. He speaks of

> Basilisks, of cannon, culverin . . .[1]

The basilisk was a light gun, of perhaps two inch calibre: the cannon themselves, because of their enormous weight, were used either for defence of walls, or in sieges for battering them down. The culverin was just light enough for field use. At the Battle of Nieuport 1600 all three armies totalling some 26,000 men, could only muster twelve or fourteen guns in all.[2] We can readily imagine the problems of movement on the roads and tracks.

The guns indeed presented the commanders with an insuperable problem. The gunners had no opportunity of practising before a battle: because of this, and the uncertain nature of the powder, anything might happen to the projectiles. It would have been suicidal to position them in the rear of the main body of troops. Therefore they had to be stationed well out on one flank or the other. But once in position their great weight and primitive carriages made them difficult to move. Even the comparatively light culverin, which threw a 16 lb ball, required a team of twenty-four animals to move it, and more in bad weather.

The effective range of cannon was low. For battering walls it was between seven and eight score paces. In spite of various projectiles in the form of rudimentary shells, chain shot,[3] and dice shot, the range against infantry was little more. The guns on the flank would be good for a single round only, if there were a body of determined cavalry against them: for after firing the gun had to be sponged out,[4] reloaded

---

[1] *1 Henry IV* II.3.54: *cf.* Kipling:
> 'Farewell Romance!' the soldier spoke,
> 'By sleight of sword we may not win,
> But scuffle 'mid uncleanly smoke
> Of arquebus and culverin . . .'

[2] Webb *op. cit.* p. 127.

[3] As in Donne: 'By him, as by chain'd shot, whole ranks do die.'

[4] In the Indian Mutiny a lucky shot smashed the sponging ram-rods of two rebel guns; this put them completely out of action, for the black powder made them foul each time they were fired. Naval gunnery produced an effective drill for this process. An admirable account 'though of much later date' of the movement and working of a twelve-pounder is given in C. S. Forester's *The Gun*.

A NOTE ON SHAKESPEARE'S ARMY

from the muzzle, returned to its original position (for it would have recoiled eight or ten feet) and re-sighted before it could be fired again. In the interval cavalry could easily over-run the gunners. Against infantry in the open the guns were ineffective:

> only before the fight do [they] trouble men: the which impediments the footmen easily auoide, eyther with going kevered [in échelon] by the nature of the situation, or with falling downe upon the grounde, when they shoote: the which also by experience hath been seene not to bee nedeful, as especially to be defended from greate ordinance, the which cannot in such wise bee leuelled, because yf they gowe highe, thei touche thee not, and if they go lowe, thei will not come nere thee.[1]

The image of the 'blank' and 'level' seems to have struck Shakespeare. There are many allusions: in *Hamlet*, in *Pericles*, and most notably in *A Winter's Tale*:

> For the harlot king
> Is quite beyond mine arm, out of the blank
> And level of my brain, plot-proof.[2]

and in *Henry VIII* (where the metaphor is more abstract):

> I stood i' the level
> Of a full-charg'd confederacy, and give thanks
> To him that chok'd it.[3]

But on all sides the gunner's task was far from simple. His cannon tapered from breach to muzzle; one of his first tasks was to ascertain whether it had been truly cast or bored, and to find the axis of his barrel: for this would not be the same as the apparent 'level' of the gun. The difference was known as the *dispart*, and was arrived at by some complex mathematical calculations. When these were completed a piece of straw bedded in wax was fixed to the muzzle to form a front sight. The elevation was obtained (in theory at least) with the help of a

---

[1] Whitehorne, *op. cit.*
[2] II.3.5. Compare Sonnet 117:
> Bring me within the level of your frown
> But shoot not at me in your waken'd hate.
[3] I.2.2.

quadrant, and if the enemy cavalry were considerate enough to allow a couple of ranging shots, the gunner might get a fair idea of how his piece threw. These ranging shots would enable him to extemporize a crude back-sight, also made of a piece of straw embedded in wax and affixed to the breech.

There were other hazards. The casting of cannon was a dangerous business at the best of times, because of air liable to be trapped in the vertical mould.[1] Flaws were frequent. The amount of powder required was large; even the small nine-pounder required nine pounds of powder per round. Cannon were weighed to determine the theoretical size of the charge. But in battle the powder and shot would be dumped in the rear of the guns; the powder in broached casks. Some form of fire, a brazier, a linstock or heated iron, was necessary to ignite the powder through the touch-hole. The military writers have much to say about safety precautions, both for the guns and for the 'shot' of the infantry, who also had open casks in the rear at which they could re-charge their powder-flasks. So Markham:

> I once knew a drunken Canoniere who upon the discharge of a Peece throwing his Linstocke into a barrell of poulder which stood behind him, blew up both himself, the whole poope of the Shippe and diuers others which were about him . . . The like happened at the besedging of the Forte at Brest in Brittany and diuers braue gentlemen were burned and spoyled . . .

VI

Most of the warfare in Shakespeare consists of sieges and battles. The best known instances are Othello's narrative:

> Of hair-breadth 'scapes i' the imminent deadly breach[2]

and Henry V's speech before Harfleur.[3] The breach might be made in

---

[1] 'Brazen' cannon are being cast at the opening of *Hamlet*: brass and iron were also used. An earlier English expedition into France halted for a time at Caen, in order to cast their artillery for the campaign in the market-place of the town.
[2] *Othello* 1.3.136.
[3] III.11.1.

A NOTE ON SHAKESPEARE'S ARMY

several ways, and all assaults were hazardous. The wall might be undermined by tunnelling, and Cornish and Welsh miners formed a unit under the Mine-Master for this purpose. The speed of movement as the ghost flits under and above the battlements suggest to Hamlet the 'pioner' who worked so quickly underground. A reference in *Othello* suggests that pioneers were extremely tough.[1]

The second method, hazardous against experienced defenders, was the attack by battering ram, enormous metal-headed beams[2] swung from a sort of overhead gantry, itself roofed in to protect the attackers from overhead fire from the walls.

The third method was attack by artillery, and, given suitable conditions, was effective. During the Irish wars it was reported that no castle could stand against cannon shot provided that the assailants had sufficient artillery, and, even more important, were able to place it in position. But Irish castles were less strongly built than those of England or the Low Countries. To make the breach the guns were deployed as close to the target as possible, subject to the range of the guns and that of the defensive fire with muskets, arrows and cannon. Webb gives illustrations of the methods of employing artillery fire: either by guns firing at the same mark from different angles, or employing cross-fire at different points on the castle walls. The guns would be protected either by earthworks or by bundles of wood packed with earth (fascines) and were always vulnerable to sorties from the defenders, who would spike the guns by driving large nails into the touch-holes. But the process of battering by artillery seems to have been a slow one. We may quote from Sir Roger Williams' *Actions in the Lowe Countries* (1618):

> After some 7000 shot, the breach was reasonable, as the assailants thought. But in truth it was not, for aboue foure foot of the ground of the rampier (rampart) was nothing battered, but falsely covered with the ruins of the parapet and the earth that fell from the highest points of the breach. Also they were faine to giue their assaults on Pontons and such engines; which they had made against reason, to adventure men against a place defended with any valour. For such a breach (be it neuer so assaultable) having many

[1] III.3.346.
[2] It is possible, though I have no evidence, that the triple-headed ram is one source of Donne's image 'Batter my heart, three-person'd God'. . .

handes to defend it with any valour, lightly is neuer entered; in case they within be of any judgement . . . and hauing earth to entrench themselues . . . For at those assaults they lost divers of their best Captaines, and at least 1600 of their brauest soldiers.

We can imagine the scene: the broken wall, the narrow passage encumbered with rubble, and the assault under the defenders' fire. It is no wonder that Othello boasted to Desdemona of his exploits.

VII

'Shot on Horseback'

Falstaff. . . . and that sprightly Scot of Scots, Douglas, that runs o'horseback up a hill perpendicular.
Prince. He that rides at high speed and with his pistol kills a sparrow flying.
Falstaff. You have hit it.
Prince. So did he never the sparrow.[1]

The case of Douglas and his pistol is worth attention. On the surface it is of course a deflation of the 'hot termagant Scot', the *miles gloriosus*, the braggart, who is a recurrent comic figure. It is paralleled by the deflation of Owen Glendower for his assumption of magical powers. But it does bring up the question of the pistol and the pistolier in Shakespeare's army.

A firelock pistol for a horseman was a contradiction in terms. The feat of supporting a heavy weapon with one hand and manipulating the burning fuse with the other would have been formidable. For night work the glow from the match would – as with any similar mechanism – betray the soldier; for assassinations the spark and the sulphurous smell of the smouldering cord would be disadvantageous. One exception was the ingenious device in which a pistol barrel was built in to the boss of a small shield; the firer, sighting through a small grid aperture, could manipulate his firelock behind cover. These 'shield-pistols' are extremely rare. The flintlock pistol did not come into common use till the mid-seventeenth century. It is just possible that Pistol's weapon –

[1] *1 Henry IV* II.4.349.

A NOTE ON SHAKESPEARE'S ARMY

For I can take, and Pistol's cock is up,
And flashing fire will follow.[1]

was a snaphance,[2] a primitive form of flintlock: in which the pan and the striking surface were separate units. But the first really practical hand-gun, which seems to have been invented in Germany in the early part of the sixteenth century, was the wheel-lock pistol.[3] Its action was rapid and reasonably waterproof. Basically it consisted of a lock in which a powerful internal spring was set up by a spanner, and held in tension by a scear. When released by the trigger it revolved a finely-toothed wheel, very much on the model of the modern cigarette-lighter. This in turn pressed against a piece of iron pyrites, held in the vice of the jaws of the cock, which itself could be moved backwards into the firing position immediately over the wheel. When the wheel revolved it automatically opened a pan which contained the priming powder. A shower of spark from the pyrites fell into it to ignite the main charge.

The lock was complicated, almost watchmakers' work, and therefore expensive; the product of the skill and invention of German and northern Italian gunsmiths. Leonardo da Vinci produced a drawing of a wheel-lock. By the early seventeenth century the pistols, fowling-pieces and rifles using this form of ignition were fairly common, but they were too expensive for general military use. As early as 1523 the city of Ferrara had published an ordinance against... 'an especially dangerous kind of firearms which are called vulgarly stone guns (wheel-locks) with which a homicide can easily be committed'. The earliest English wheel-lock pistol dates from about 1580.[4]

But the point about the wheel-lock, and 'that sprightly Scot of Scots', was that it revolutionized the use of cavalry against the hitherto

[1] *Henry V* II.1.54. Earlier Falstaff had said that he would 'double-charge' Pistol with honours; in any event a risky proceeding.
[2] So called from the supposed resemblance of the 'cock' to the motion of a pecking fowl.
[3] It is of interest to note that there was a total embargo on selling, firing or making pistols within two miles of the person of Queen Elizabeth. (Boynton, *op. cit.* p. 119).
[4] Peterson, *op. cit.* pp. 66, 67. These are *not* the 'stone guns' described on p. 79.

formidable opposition of the pikeman's 'steel-tipped wood'. It was now possible for well-trained horsemen to gallop up to the enemy lines, fire one or two pistols at a convenient range to allow successive ranks to repeat the maneouvre, while the first ranks galloped off to reload. The common calibre was relatively small, twenty bullets to the pound:[1] no doubt for the sake of lightness, and diminished recoil. The dialogue which we have quoted from *1 Henry IV* has an important aspect: not only was Douglas a superb horseman who could attack over unfavourable ground, but whatever the exaggeration, he was an excellent pistolier. The myth of the sparrow is not irrelevant. The frontispiece shows such a 'shot on horseback' in action. We may note the large spherical knob on the end of the butt. This was a common feature of heavy pistols in the eighteenth century; at times the whole weapon was made of metal, and could be used effectively as a small club. This lends point to the description of Dr. Johnson knocking his opponent down (in controversy) with the butt end of his pistol if the weapon misfired.

VIII

It seems as if insufficient attention has been paid to the 'gentlemen' and their function in Shakespeare's Army. Webb[2] mentions them, but as 'gentlemen of the company', citing Digges' *Stratiocos* and Garrard's *Arte of Warre*. Other writers, including Markham, are less approving of the

> rash, inconsiderate, fiery voluntaries[3]

These men received no pay. They were in the ranks but not of them:

> a ranke of men which voluntarily and out of their own meere motion doe betake themselves into the Warres, grounding the strength of their desires thereunto, upon some vertuous and honest purpose.

---

[1] We may note that the same method is still used for classifying the bores of modern shot-guns: *e.g.* a sixteen bore is a weapon whose barrel diameter is shown by sixteen spherical balls to the pound.
[2] Webb, *op. cit.* p. 82.
[3] *King John* II.1.67.

A NOTE ON SHAKESPEARE'S ARMY

They provided their own clothing, arms and equipment. They could choose the captain or general under whom they wished to serve, but seem to have been under no legal discipline,

> neither are they tied to any strictness of any particular dutie, but as free and noble gentlemen may bestow their horses in any honourable fashion[1] . . . they may challenge in all Marches the most honourable and principall place of the Battell.

These 'honourable places' included outposts and 'flying picquets', the visiting of sentries. They were given the password of the day, and it was their duty to attempt to surprise sleepy sentries. They could themselves claim sentry-duties on royal or important occasions, such as the watch on the battlements of Elsinore. Marcellus, Bernardo and Francisco are not officers, but, to judge from their conversations with Hamlet and Horatio, are clearly not common soldiers. They were armed with the ceremonial partizans.[2] But the motives of the 'gentlemen' in joining the army were certainly mixed:

> . . . Some by their own ambition, some by their wiues, and some (as they say Dogges goe to Church) onely for company, without either a noble end, or almost a tolerable Purpose, for as they were led by vaine glory . . . hence it hath come to passe that I haue knowne divers discreet Generalls . . . which haue proclaimed that no man (upon paine of Death) . . . without his speciall licence . . . should either inroll himself or else to depart from the armie: by which means the multitude of Voluntaries are lessened.

We may well imagine that the Voluntaries objected strongly to 'passing the musters' and being placed under strict military law. Another passage makes plain their ill repute:

> . . . in these our latter succeeding times, when Generals haue (out of popularitie) been less sparing of Honour, and more prodigall in bestowing all manner of martiall bounties, so that the mixture being wonderfully unproper, and the Priueledges which they assume needlesse . . . they haue bred such confusion that in Marching, Fighting, Lodging, nay not so much but in Victualling they haue rather brought forth the fruits of Trouble and Disorder,

[1] We may think, perhaps, of the position of a Fellow-Commoner in a Cambridge college of the eighteenth century.
[2] I.I.40.

105

than either ease or perfection to anie parte of the Armie . . . In one seruice I saw a whole afternoone spent (by excellent Commanders) in putting two hundred Voluntaries into order, and yet all labour lost, nor was at anie time seene to the number of fiftie that stood in their true places. I haue seene them also when they haue been to march into the field, so husled for want of knowledge where to place themselves or their vassals, and so offensive to the Generall by an indecent crowding and thronging about him, that the particular Officers of the Field, as the Scout-master and Corporalls of the Field were neither able to approach to receive direction,[1] nor yet able to passe into the Armie, to deliuer advertisements.[2]

Gervase Markham's experiences ring true, and has obviously embittered him. We may quote another view of the problems of morale raised by the presence of Voluntaries:

. . . the Colonel must not only use and treat them with an advantage in their pay, but also feast them, cherish them, and set them oftentimes by course at his own table, and always show them a courteous countenance, with which show of friendly courtesy soldiers be incredibly fed, and contrarywise, marvelous displeased with the haughty looks of proud disdain.[3]

The description in the last sentence fits Coriolanus admirably. No term of abuse is too violent for the Romans who were beaten back to their trenches in the first assault.[4] In his view it is clearly the voluntaries who have saved the day:

> but for our gentlemen,
> The common file – a plague! tribunes for them! –
> The mouse ne'er shunn'd the cat as they did budge
> From rascals worse than they.[5]

Marcius gives them the credit for the successful counter-attack.

In the organization of the company the 'file' in Shakespeare's view would have consisted of ten men, and the gentlemen would have formed

---

[1] The modern 'Order Group'?
[2] The transmission of orders downwards by the officers. Perhaps the word 'advertisement' has also an overtone of warning.
[3] Digges *cit.* in Webb *op. cit.* p. 82.
[4] I.4.30.
[5] I.6.42.

A NOTE ON SHAKESPEARE'S ARMY

files of their own; much as in World War I certain companies were formed privately of friends or companions. (This was disastrous, for many of them swore not to accept commissions, and in the 1914–15 period, great numbers of potential officers were lost). As of right, this file or files could, as we have seen, claim the most honourable positions in the battle: hence the subsequent allusion of Menenius:

> This is strange now: do you two know how you are censured here in the city; I mean of us o'the right-hand file?[1]

Perhaps there were political overtones as well.

IX

It is not easy to form a clear picture of the organization of the Elizabethan Army. There are several reasons why this should be so. Armies were raised on a basis that contained elements of improvisation, made still more irregular by corruption and by political considerations. The strength of units and their weaponry varied in accordance with what was available (whether by importation from the Low Countries, or from the government factories); even more important, by conditions of finance. The science of war was changing rapidly, and there was a conflict between the 'New Army' type of officer, learned in the new military theories, and the older officers who had had battle experience. This is pointed up by the Cassio-Iago situation. We miss much unless we realize this, and the fact that the ensign or ancient of the Company was an office of the highest responsibility and trust. There is thus some humour in the unwarranted assumption by Pistol of that rank. On the other hand, Othello put Iago in charge of Desdemona's escort to Cyprus; the supreme measure of his confidence in his 'honesty'.

At the same time we should realize the traditional enmity and rivalry between the lieutenant and the ensign in the company structure. Cassio is described by Iago as 'a mere arithmetician'; some at least of the Globe audience would have realized that senior officers were expected to be able to extract cube roots in order to set up the 'Battell' correctly, and that the gibe was one aimed at the new-type staff-officer. Gower is

[1] 2.I.24

THE LIVING IMAGE

a 'goot captain, and is good knowledge and literatured in the wars';[1] but from Fluellen's approval of him it is likely that his reading had been in the Greek and Roman classics rather than in the books of the new science.

Several critics have queried the concern of Othello, an army commander, with the details of organization at company level involved in the Cassio-Iago quarrel. I can only suggest that Cyprus, though of great political importance, was a relatively small command, and that possibly the military government was on a company basis. In such circumstances the general would have been particularly concerned for the morale of his staff, and the personal problems common among officers who are mainly concerned with administration rather than with fighting.

We miss something of the comedy unless we realize that Falstaff's promotion of Pistol to lieutenant was quite unwarranted; as was that of Bardolph to corporal. For this rank we may quote Gervase Markham:

> This Corporal ought to be a man carefully chosen out, and endued with valour, virtue, diligence and experience; he ought to be of reverend and grave years, thereby to draw on respect, but withal of a sound judgement; for experience without it, is like a jewel at the bottom of the sea, which neither adorns itself nor others; he must be a cherisher of virtue, and a lover of concord, for he is said to be the father of his squadron, and must therefore love them and provide for them as for his natural children.[2]

There are other comic ironies. The looting for which Nym was executed was regarded by the troops as a legitimate activity, and, indeed, the dominant reason for engaging in the various expeditions. At Agincourt every tenth file was provided with a large iron-shod maul or hammer with which to crack, as if they were lobsters, the armour of the dead knights in order to get at their rich clothes.[3] The ransom of captured officers was an important source of income; as were also the 'dead pays', ten per cent (even in peace-time) of the nominal company strength, for whose 'shadows' the company commander drew pay and allowances. There was thus comedy in Falstaff's assertion that 'he had

---
[1] *Henry V* IV.7.147.
[2] *Five Decades of Epistles of War.*
[3] 'Bowmen's Battle': 'Weston Martyr', *op. cit.*

A NOTE ON SHAKESPEARE'S ARMY

led his ragamuffins where they are peppered',[1] so that only three of his company were left; the audience would have realized that Falstaff would have been greatly enriched after the Battle of Shrewsbury. Jorgensen points out that he is shown as far more prosperous (but not to the extent of a thousand pounds) after that event.

We may miss, too, the topical nature of the description of the comic Irish captain of *Henry V*, Macmorris. His speech seems to me improbable – as contrasted with Fluellen, whose Welsh intonations and rhythms are wholly genuine – and he is notably bloodthirsty. The Irish captains, as Jorgensen points out,[2] were notorious for being cut-throats as well as 'unlearned' in war. They were, in fact, an actual embarrassment in the service. In 1598 Elizabeth wrote to the Council in Ireland 'that you do use all convenient measures to clear our army of the Irish'.

Among the 'irregular humourists' of the history plays Pistol is not merely the traditional *miles gloriosus* of the Latin comedy (with a taste for Marlovian rhetoric) but the classic type of military 'spiv'. As with all armies the quartermaster services were liable to become objects of suspicion and even hatred; they were often the cause of mutiny. Pistol's rank, we have noted, as lieutenant appears to be wholly irregular, as is Falstaff's dangerous promise to 'double-charge him with honours'. Falstaff's own command is a piece of favouritism on the part of the Prince:

Prince Henry. I have procured thee, Jack, a charge of foot.
Falstaff.   I would it had been of horse.[3]

Pistol adds to his prospective villainies by suggesting that he will join the rear échelon and make his fortune among the civilian rabble, the 'poys and the baggage', that attended all Tudor expeditionary forces, and in which the entrepreneurs frequently discounted at a large profit the promissory notes of the pay of the fighting troops:

> For I shall sutler be
> Unto the camp, and profits will accrue.[4]

[1] *1 Henry IV* v.3.36.
[2] Jorgensen *op. cit.* p. 78ff.
[3] *1 Henry IV* III.3.193.
[4] *Henry V* II.1.112.

THE LIVING IMAGE

We may notice certain other features of the Army. Jorgensen and others have discussed the apparent absence of any ranks between those of general and captain. It may be that Shakespeare found it dramatically inappropriate to introduce these ranks, or that his practical knowledge was limited to the Company, or that his sources demanded, in the main, generals and captains. Let us consider the larger picture of the organization.

The army commander was usually a royal personage. Below him, and serving as his deputy, was the Lord (or High-) Marshal, sometimes known as the Sergeant-General or – confusingly – as the Sergeant-Major-General. Below him in the war establishment there would be Lieutenant-Generals commanding the horse and foot respectively, and a Quarter-master General, perhaps roughly equivalent to the Chief Administrative Officer today. Under him come the Wagon-master, the Forage-master, and the Victual-master, as well as the Master Gunner. On the General Staff side there were four 'Corporals of the Field,' their rank apparently between that of captain and colonel. One each was responsible for the three main divisions of the 'Battell', the 'vaward', 'Battell' (the main body) and rearguard respectively; the fourth was presumably 'spare', for communication or perhaps reconnaissance duties. Additional officers were the Captain of Pioneers, the Scout Master, the Judge-Marshal, with the Provost-Marshal and his Deputy. On the 'A' side of the staff were the Treasurer and the Muster-Master.

If the army were operating on a regimental basis – regiments were usually known by the names of their commanding officers – the staff would comprise the colonel, a lieutenant-colonel, a sergeant-major and a 'colonel's lieutenant'; the strength in theory being five companies each of two hundred men. Organization into divisions is a much later growth. The company organization included the captain, lieutenant and ensign (ancient), with a clerk, a surgeon, a harbenger, and two each of drums and fifes. These, as described in the next section, were essential for transmission of orders as well as for stirring Othello's martial spirits. Of the company officers, the 'Captain's Squadron' and the 'Lieutenant's Squadron' were pikemen (an indication of the importance attached to the weapon), while the musket squadrons were in charge of the ancient and a sergeant. It is not clear what command the 'bleeding sergeant' of

A NOTE ON SHAKESPEARE'S ARMY

Macbeth held, for there were four allotted to each company. The squadrons were formed of 'camarados' or sections, of varying strength. Gervase Markham gives only two per squadron, which supposing ten or twelve men to a 'camarado', does not agree with a company strength of two hundred odd. Comparative weapon strengths for different companies are shown in the following tables:

Company of 100	*Company of 150*
15 Muskets	23 Muskets
15 Calivers	22 Calivers
10 Halberdiers	15 Halberdiers
50 Pikemen	75 Pikemen
10 'Dead Pays'	15 'Dead Pays'

The number of pikemen in relation to the 'shot' is an indication of the relative expense, both in initial cost of their weapons and in that of the powder and bullets to train them. This was a perennial source of trouble to the authorities in time of peace. The 'shot' who had had no opportunities for target practice would be worse than useless: there are constant complaints of the inability of the soldiers to hit the proverbial barn door at a hundred yards. But there was a further political dilemma, which is not unfamiliar; it was highly dangerous to allow the troops to have free access to their weapons. If they kept them at home, they were damaged, or rusted; and the situation was not much better in the central armouries organized on a county basis. This left unsolved the double problem of illicit retention of arms (and the consequent threat of rebellion), and the need for legitimate but expensive exercise in them.

X

'The spirit-stirring drum . . .'

It is common knowledge that the armies of the Elizabethan stage were differentiated by what we may call the signature-tunes, on trumpet, fife and drum, of their commanders; and that this did in fact add another dimension to the battle scenes. Little attention has been given to the drum. The establishment of drummers seems to have been four per company, and two for what would now be called the Headquarters Company.

They had many duties. Drums and trumpets were used to mark the watches on board ship; on land for reveillé, 'beating to quarters', various parades. A drummer accompanied the guard that relieved the sentries at dawn, so that we have the exquisite passage from Spenser:

> The knight much wond'red at his sudden wit,
> And said, 'The term of life is limited,
> Ne may a man prolong, nor shorten it:
> The soldier may not move from watchful stead,
> Nor leave his stand until his captain bid.'
> 'Who life did limit by Almighty doom,'
> Quoth he, 'knows best the terms establishèd;
> And he, that 'points the sentinel his room,
> Doth license him depart at sound of morning drum.'[1]

Of the evening drum, I think that the image at the end of Bishop King's *Exequy* may be that of the vanguard, with the harbenger, the officer responsible for billeting, coming wearily to their evening rest. The war-imagery is sustained:

> 'Tis true, with shame and grief I yield,
> Thou like the *Vann* first took'st the field,
> And gotten hast the victory
> In thus adventuring to die
> Before me, whose more years might crave
> A just precedence in the grave.
> But heark! My Pulse, like a soft Drum
> Beats my approach, tells *Thee* I come;
> And slow howere my marches be,
> I shall at last sit down by *Thee*.

'The Victory' is from *I Corinthians* xv ('But thanks be to God which giveth us the victory'); the pulse-beat is soft, muffled by old age. But at the end of the march he will not *lie* by his wife's body in the grave; he will sit, as a weary soldier in some house or inn.

---

[1] *Faerie Queene* I,ix.xli.

A NOTE ON SHAKESPEARE'S ARMY

It seems that individual commanders had their personal drum music. Volumia says

> Methinks I hear hither your husband's drum'[1]

The French General on the walls of Bordeaux –

> Hark! hark! the Dauphin's drum, a warning bell
> Sings heavy music to thy timorous soul.[2]

In *Lear* a drum precedes the challenge of the Herald's trumpet:

> Let the drum strike, and prove my title thine.[3]

But the most important function of the drum was to transmit orders on the battlefield. Such control as was practicable after the battle was joined might be carried out by hand signals (liable to be ineffective in the 'fog of battle' or over uneven ground), or by word of mouth which, then as now, could be highly misleading. The drum transmitted five simple orders, which the soldiers of the company would learn: Arm, March, Troop (*i.e.* move into formation), Charge, Retreat.[4] The Company colours, borne by the ensign, were important as the rallying-point of the Company: hence the modern ceremony of Trooping the Colour. It also appears that the Captains had their own personal colours, bannerets or pikes and halberds.

XI

No one can envy the lot of the Elizabethan soldier. He was ill-paid and worse administered. His main hope of advantage lay precisely in the loot that Henry V's famous edict forbade. If he were mutilated he was left 'to beg at the town's end'. It is true that there were surgeons to attend him in battle, but their equipment was both rudimentary and nightmarish. In sieges, in marches, and in battles he was subject to every sort of disease. The line of archers at Agincourt were badly affected by dysentry. On the march, a typical ration was 'a pound of

[1] *Coriolanus* 1.3.30.
[2] *I Henry VI* IV.2.39.
[3] V.3.82.
[4] Cruickshank, *op. cit.* p. 192.

bisket and a Poore-John[1] between two men for one day'. The soldier received as pay 8d a day, 4/8d a week: he received 'lendings' in cash at the rate of 3/- per week, the balance of 1/8d being in theory credited to him against a 'reckoning' that was – again in theory – to be held at intervals of six months 'between the Prince and euery Souldier'. It is little wonder that the Generals and Princes were so constantly hard-pressed to find the soldiers' pay. But out of his 'lendings'[2] the soldier had also to pay for his rations – 4d a day for food and 1d a day for drink: so that his spending money was one penny per week. Normal rations were

> Two daies flesh and either Beefe or Bacon for Sundaies and Thursdaies: two daies butter as on Monday and Tuesday; one day Chese as Wednesday; and two daies fish as Friday and Saturday.'

For quantity, on a bacon day, for example, a man would get one and a half pounds of bread and half a pound of bacon. As in all services, mutinies were apt to arise out of the poor quality of the food and the 'Victuall-masters'' practice of keeping back the best rations for themselves, and issuing the worst to the troops.

The Elizabethan Army was thus a mass of paradoxes. Shakespeare depicts Williams and Bates as rank-and-file men arguing sensibly and profoundly with their disguised king. Fluellen, Jamy and Macmorris are professional soldiers, and educated men. The wars (as in the Bible)[3] were strictly seasonal. Markham tells us

> I was euer a lover of the Muses, and as I spent my Summer Progresse in the warres, so I consumed my Winters quiet with wholesome delights of forraine Academies . . .

---

[1] 'Poore-John' – salt cod, often ancient. See the description of Caliban in *The Tempest*, II.2.22.

[2] This is the point of the allusion by Bolingbroke in *Richard II*:
> Look, what I speak, my life shall prove it true;
> That Mowbray hath received eight thousand nobles
> In name of lendings for your highness' soldiers,
> The which he hath detain'd for lewd employments. . .
>   (I.1.87)

[3] *2 Samuel* 11.1. 'And it came to pass, after the year was expired, at the time when kings go forth to battle'. . .

A NOTE ON SHAKESPEARE'S ARMY

Even in the midst of a campaign Fluellen is ready for professional military discussion:

> I beseech you now will you voutsafe me, look you, a few disputations with you, a party touching or concerning the disciplines of the war, the Roman wars, in the way of argument, look you, and friendly communication . . .[1]

The books would have probably been Caesar's *Gallic War* and the *Commentaries*; perhaps Xenophon; the campaigns of Philip of Macedon; Machiavelli's newly-translated *Art of Warre*, Garrard's *Art of Warre*, Digges' *Stratioticos*; some of the many accounts of the sixteenth-century campaigns in the Low Countries in which professional soldiers sought – with some impartiality as to loyalties – experience and profit.[2]

XI

But who can doubt that it is in what we should now call the politico-military world that Shakespeare's insight into character, action and motive remains supreme, and perennial? These, and the principles of war, remain relatively constant. We can translate so much into modern terms. *Antony and Cleopatra* underlines, not only the problems of a tripartite command, but those of the aging soldier and his sexual 'dotage'. Hotspur in modern times might be the dashing and irresponsible commander of an Armoured Division. From one angle (there are many) *Troilus and Cressida* is an exposition of quarrels between allies, the frustration of plans, the arrogance and petulance of great commanders, the boredom and sexuality of prolonged and aimless war.[3] In *Othello* we have the problem of a Commanding General's staff: its jealousies and frictions; the influence of the wives of Senior Officers, and even of prostitutes; the aimless quarrelling of soldiers in their cups. And for the arrogance and self-centredness of a great soldier, confronted with democracies that he does not pretend to understand, and problems of civil life

---

[1] *Henry V* 3.3.96.
[2] For a discussion, see Webb, *op. cit.* Ch. VIII.
[3] It was not mere caprice that a production of the play in modern dress showed Thersites as a hard-bitten and disillusioned war-correspondent.

with which he is unable to cope,[1] there is the example of Coriolanus. In an age when military appointments were largely political, and private armies were relatively common, the risks of rebellion as well as the mishandling of troops were intensified. Yet for all these military vices it would be possible to offer for each one not but several *exempla* from the Second World War.

And finally Shakespeare has much to tell us of the folly of war, the contention for an 'eggshell', the nature of capricious tyranny, the lust for power; above all of the nature of *hubris*, the sin of pride, the failure to keep station in the complex hierarchies; the failure of strategical and political judgement when we are blinded by the just or unjust gods. But behind the trumpets, tuckets, the marching and countermarchings, the 'outrageous cannon', the knights and the prancing horses, there is, somewhere, Shakespeare's image of the Common Soldier, and for it we may again turn to Gervase Markham:

> This let him learn to know, this let him learn to endure, and this will make all hazards familiar. To conclude, as to this life of a Soldier both belong all the miseries that can be conceived: so to the same must be fixed as an armour,[2] the greatest patience that ever was professed; so shall our Soldier be victorious every way, and all the vices of baseness, rashness, murther, robbery, ravishment, folly, dullness, riot, deceit, pride and covetousness, which like so many infections lurk about armies, shall as disperst clouds fly from his presence, and leave him to the world beloved and admired.[3]

[1] The chapter in Professor Jorgenson's book. 'From the casque to the cushion' is particularly illuminating. (Ch. VI, *op. cit.*)
[2] *cf.* 'the armature of S. Paul', *Ephesians* VI 13.
[3] *Five Decades of Epistles of Warre*, 1622.

CHAPTER 8

The Images of 'Antony and Cleopatra'

It has always seemed to me that great literature at its greatest intensity displays the sage, the lover, or some images of despair, and that these are traditional attitudes.

W. B. YEATS, *1930 Diary*

I

Antony and Cleopatra is a strange play, over which endless controversy has raged, and I think it is important that we should come to it (as indeed to all plays at all times) with a completely open mind. For it raises certain moral issues which I was forced to consider, in a peculiar manner, early in my teaching career. A pupil – admittedly from overseas – threatened to sue me and/or the Faculty Board of English for 'allowing or prescribing or causing to be prescribed' the play *Antony and Cleopatra*, which, he alleged, was calculated to corrupt the mind and morals of any student who was forced, under duress of examinations, to read it. There is no need to apologize now on that particular count. But the incident may cause us to sit back and think for a moment; and then we hear the voice of another Puritan of our times, denouncing the play more elegantly but no less violently:

> Shakespeare finally strains all his huge command of rhetoric and stage pathos to give a tragic sublimity to the whole wretched business, and to persuade foolish spectators that the world was well lost by the twain.

The voice is Bernard Shaw's. At the root of it there is, of course, the old Platonic indictment; and we can almost hear Stubbes or Gosson licking their lips, and appealing to the Authorities of the City that such plays

THE LIVING IMAGE

neither in polity nor in religion . . . are to be suffered in a Christian Commonwealth, specially being of that frame and matter as usually they are, containing nothing but profane fables, lascivious matters, cozening devices, and scurrilous behaviours, which are so set forth as that they move wholly to imitation and not the avoiding of those faults and vices which they represent.

'Profane fables' – of the great heroes that welcome suicide, and couch in flowers in the Elysian meadows, and greet the ghost of their mistress's handmaid with a kiss:

> . . . mistake by the way
> The maid, and tell the mistress of that delay.

'Lascivious matters', where sensuality endures and is magnified under the Egyptian sun; where generals reel drunken from a political dinner; where a great queen stoops to deceive her conqueror over her household jewelry. True enough, maybe; but then we ask (putting on our furred gowns) how does it come about that an immoral heathen play, that glorifies whoredom, desertion, and suicide, in which the hero can say to a woman whom he has lately called 'triple-turned whore' –

> I am dying, Egypt, dying; only
> I here importune death awhile, until
> Of many thousand kisses the poor last
> I lay upon thy lips.[1]

– how and why is this play the most greatly loved and perhaps the most moving of all the great tragedies? Dr. Johnson (who stooped unerringly on the play's moral weakness) or Rhymer or Collier might have found a 'moral gesture' to approve. 'The business of plays is to show men what they should do by showing them on the stage doing what they should not.' But here we seem to be ranging in open country outside morality; just as we are outside and beyond almost every one of the received canons of dramatic theory. We break all the laws of time and place; we tear Plutarch to shreds, or paraphrase him, as the mood takes us. And still the thing remains, a miracle of poetry; greater poetry, taken all in all, than in any other play. Even if (with me) you confess

[1] IV.12.18.

THE IMAGES OF 'ANTONY AND CLEOPATRA'

your own barbarousness, there is no escaping a great stirring of the heart. Why, exactly? And what is *Antony and Cleopatra* all about?

II

From one point of view we may think of it as a sort of fairy-tale; if you please, a common wish-fulfillment. The myth of a man's Indian summer of love, the recovery of youth and virility by a grey-haired soldier, scarred with battle, is an image of a larger dream. There are few men over forty who never think longingly of that cauldron of Medea, or of women whose sexual attractiveness remains unimpaired by custom or by age. Before Eve was Lilith: the eternal image of desire perpetually kindled, perpetually unsatisfied. Superimposed on this we might find a second fairy tale; of the great warrior, armoured by his love for the battle, who goes out to confront defeat; and, seemingly, to die for the news of his beloved's death. The great passages of the play can be quoted in support. On the barge, every image (the swollen sails, the beaten gold, the beaten water, the cupids who fan their mistresses) reflects its sultry sensuality. Enobarbus must leave Plutarch's flattened prose, and invoke an image of a woman beyond the vision of Rubens or Titian. The splendour of the language supports us in our dream:

> To this great fairy I'll commend thy acts,
> Make her thanks bless thee. O thou day o' the world!
> Chain mine arm'd neck; leap thou, attire and all,
> Through proof of harness to my heart, and there
> Ride on the pants triumphing.
> *Cleopatra.*   Lord of lords!
> O infinite virtue! com'st thou smiling from
> The world's great snare uncaught?[1]

III

Yet the fairy tale is humanized (and made brutal too) at every turn. No language can be too bitter to describe Cleopatra: in the mouths of

[1] IV.8.12.

Rome, of Antony's staff, of Antony himself. She is the 'triple-turned whore'; her lust is a gypsy's. She can drink Antony to bed, mock him, behave like a spoilt prima donna. Her jealousy of Octavia, her sharp enquiries about every detail of her person, is classical (and very feminine) in its ferocity. When Dryden came to rewrite the play he was quick to re-organize it to take advantage of that situation, and to confront the Virtuous Wife and the Mistress in the quadrilateral structure of antipathies and of piquant abuse so dear to the Restoration. She has the temper, and sometimes the language, of a virago. It is common practice in the East to reward the bringer of evil tidings with beating, mutilation or death; but even Cleopatra's women cringe before her rages when they venture to tease her:

> By Isis, I will give thee bloody teeth,
> If thou with Caesar paragon again
> My prince of men.[2]

That they love her, these girls who ape her cunning in love, is clear, but it does not emerge fully till the end. And the abuse of her strengthens in Antony's own mouth:

> The foul Egyptian has betrayed me . . .
> Triple-turn'd whore, 'tis thou![2]

IV

Lust has blinded and tamed him to Cleopatra's whims. She has the feminine characteristics, the capricious temper, of the hawk. Antony's mind passes with that thought to the terrible image of the hawk with its seeled eyes. Cleopatra has 'been a *boggler* ever' – the hawk that does not select and keep to one quarry, but turns backwards and forwards from one to another as she has turned from lover to lover:[3] he, like the blinded hawk, stumbles in the filth of the falconers' mews, surrounded

---
[1] I.5.69
[2] IV.10.24ff.
[3] So the irresponsible haggard of *Twelfth Night*, that 'checks at every feather/ That comes before his eye' (III.1.66).

THE IMAGES OF 'ANTONY AND CLEOPATRA'

by the jeering yard-boys who will see that she is given no sleep till she surrenders. (How cruel could the Elizabethans be?)

> You have been a boggler ever:
> But when we in our viciousness grow hard, –
> O misery on't! – the wise gods seel our eyes;
> In our own filth drop our clear judgements; make us
> Adore our errors; laugh at's while we strut
> To our confusion.[1]

Strut – is this the word – we remember *Macbeth* – of the actor, mimicking greatness, continually trying to reassure himself? Does Antony know for a moment that he has been the victim in some monstrous and cruel farce?

There is another image from the wild. One theme of the play is sexual obsession. Shakespeare describes the sea-fight at Actium. In de Herèdia's sonnet Antony, looking into Cleopatra's eyes, sees in them prophetically

> Tout un mer immense où fuyaient des galères.

This is how Scarus describes it:

> She once being loof'd,
> The noble ruin of her magic, Antony,
> Claps on his sea-wing, and like a doting mallard
> Leaving the fight in height, flies after her.[2]

There are several points to consider here. The Roman fleet has presumably got to windward of Cleopatra's Egyptian galleys. As in Nelson's day, the 'weather-gage' battle is all-important. The galleys cannot turn to windward;[3] they must up-helm and run with a following or quartering wind.

---

[1] III.11.109.
[2] III.8.27.
[3] Though some commentators on this passage suggest that this (loof'd = luffed) means that in order to flee the ships turn to windward. This is nonsense. Consider the accurate seamanship of the opening of *The Tempest*.

Antony 'claps on his sea-wing', that is, hoists the square-sails on his fleet. The word 'claps' is harsh-sounding: may it not suggest the clatter of the yards and blocks as they go up to the mast-heads? Now we have an image-vortex beginning – *claps* – *wing* – *mallard*. And may there not be a submerged pun in 'Let the Egyptians go a-ducking', from the mallards and the beaters of the brook?

In spring, beside a slow-flowing river, one can observe the antics of wild duck. Two or three mallards will pursue a single duck in courtship fights: wheeling, settling on the water, with a great quacking and clatter of wings as they take off. It is a peculiar sound, as typical as that of a woodcock rising from cover. The mallards are 'doting', obsessed with the sexual urge: the ducks, after their manner, give the impression of being embarrassed and even bored. But there is a secondary wave of this sexual excitement in the autumn: and Antony is in the autumn of his life. Aging men, and aging generals, seek reassurance in their past lives and battles, as Lear does in madness. The 'doting mallard' would have been familiar through brook-hawking; the 'boggling' hawk, 'hard' in wickedness (the image is of the Bible as well as of one of the many hawks' maladies) is used with complete spontaneity.

Antony and Cleopatra is famous for the recurrent patterning of its images. One instance of this such are the 'serpent' motifs. Among these one example has not, I think, received full attention. It involves an interesting piece of folk-lore.

In the early spring, on many rivers that flow into the Atlantic, vast quantities of thread-like fishes appear from the sea and go up stream. They are the tiny eels, some three inches long and almost transparent except for their black eyes; which have been spawned at great depths near the Sargasso sea and have made their way across the Atlantic, possibly to the river of their parents. They are often so thick in eddies that country folk can scoop them out in pails and feed them to the pigs. They are also extremely adventurous in their travels and may be found in pools of water, or on wet rocks, beside a waterfall.

It is, or was, widely believed in country districts that if one takes a piece of thick white horsehair, cuts it into lengths and soaks it in water, it will turn into an eel. This is understandable; the slightly swollen hair is not unlike an elver. Hence the otherwise obscure allusion:

THE IMAGES OF 'ANTONY AND CLEOPATRA'

> Much is breeding
> Which, like the courser's hair, hath yet but life
> And not a serpent's poison.[1]

For the imagery of the serpent, of 'Old Nile', of Egypt, of reptiles that may serve as the instruments of suicide, seem to pattern, in jest or earnest, the fabric of the play.

One last image from 'the wild':

> You ribaudred nag of Egypt,
> Whom leprosy o'ertake . . .[2]

Antony's outburst has shifted from hawk to horse. *Ribaudred* is usually glossed as 'lewd', 'wanton'. To me it suggests the old over-ridden horse that has carried many lovers (the bawdy pun is Enobarbus') but with the haggard appearance that I associate with Dürer's picture of 'Death Riding': the rib-case showing through the skin, the misery and dejection of the beast. Behind or before it there is the horse-jade pun for a light woman, whose leprosy will, like Cresseid's, be the result of her promiscuity.

V

Perhaps more terrible is the revulsion in that image that seems to often to have stirred Shakespeare's very entrails, the thought of the 'drab' as a fragment of meat, greasy and cold upon a plate:

> I found you as a morsel, cold upon
> Dead Caesar's trencher.[3]

when the word *trencher* seems to rasp harshly, steel upon wood, with all the revulsion of Shakespeare at cold, greasy food and the contempt implicit (to us at least) in the associations of 'trencher-fed' hounds. So we can turn the play in our hands, like a crystal, and find in it exaltation, degradation; Shakespeare's art, as in all the plays, is to maintain until the last, when man's greatness or weariness rises under the death-pressure,

[1] I.2.195.
[2] III.8.20.
[3] III.11.116.

THE LIVING IMAGE

just this advance and retreat of our sympathies. In this ebb and flow – have you noticed all the tide-images in the play? – we are kept in doubt to the end as to the riddle of Cleopatra herself: even under this death pressure she can jest with her women, launch her fury on Seleucus, fawn on Caesar; and then draw herself up, as it were, with the great speech

> No more, but e'en a woman –

Charmain and Iras have been calling her, in a sort of crescendo, by all her titles: Lady, Madam, Royal Egypt, Empress. Now she sheds them all:

> No more, but e'en a woman, and commanded
> By such poor passion as the maid that milks
> And does the meanest chares . . .[1]

This will be picked up, miraculously, when the asp is at her breast.

VI

But *Antony and Cleopatra* is also a play about war; the destiny of an empire and, above all, the luck of the soldier. This is, as all soldiers know, a real and a frightening thing. The ghost of Julius Caesar was no doubt stilled at Philippi. Now the triple pillars carry the Roman World. On its periphery, generals who are only a little less great than their masters must watch, politically, their own success. In the exquisite balance of the first two Acts, the scenes poised between the polar antinomies of Rome and Egypt, Shakespeare finds time to show the spreading of the ripples from the festivities of the Nile. We are aware of a sort of double trajectory of individuals and nations, and they are in part identified. In Antony's moments of crisis Cleopatra is addressed as 'Egypt'. The Nile, the Cydnus, acquire a special significance, and we remember that the rivers also are gods. Rome is distant, cold, dutiful, informed by the Roman *Virtus*; a hard, marmoreal sort of place, that breeds both Octavius Caesars, and a baying underworld of the mob. Even the battlefield is a strange one, where private soldiers talk familiarly with their generals, and make atrocious puns on their wounds: they

[1] IV.13.72.

THE IMAGES OF 'ANTONY AND CLEOPATRA'

even give perfectly sound advice – which is disregarded – on strategy:

> O noble emperor! do not fight by sea
> Trust not to rotten planks...
>   Let the Egyptians
> And the Phoenicians go a-ducking...[1]

For one scene the great Captains meet on the galley. Now for a moment the war is, as it were, in slack water. But treachery is everywhere; even the servants mock their masters' drunkenness. Antony is by turn pompous, enigmatic, laconic. Pompey suffers a strange sort of public-school morality. Menas offers to cut the cable, and slit the throats of the triumvirate. When once it is said, Pompey will have none of it:

> Ah, this thou should'st have done,
> And not have spoke on't! In me 'tis villainy;
> In thee 't had been good service. Thou must know,
> Tis not my profit that does lead mine honour;
> Mine honour, it.[2]

And because Pompey speaks thus, Menas deserts Pompey's fortunes; here again is the luck of the soldier, the eternal factor in his greatness. Menas and Enobarbus are left together, pledging each other's healths; for Enobarbus will be the second deserter. On the galley the Great Men, unbuttoned, fumbling with words, strive to build good fellowship out of drink, letting themselves go with the current of the wine. Caesar, the efficient intellectual, is merely angered and confused at his own impotence as the drink takes hold. Lepidus, the weakest, soonest carried off, hints darkly and persistently at the mysteries of the Nile; skirting the edge of the proprieties even for a General Officers' party. For the fellowship of the soldier in drink is traditional – witness that fatal guest-night in *Othello* – and it is hollow, and it is dangerous, for all the drinking songs; and one's mind turns to another conference (for so the gyres of history work) at which two thirds of the world, having drunk deep in factitious fellowship, gave away to the third sufficient of it to ensure that no peace could be established within their lifetimes ...

[1] III.7.61.
[2] II.7.79.

The galleys swing at anchor in the tide, and the wine or the vodka passes; the great commanders sing hand in hand, as at a children's party. This night revelry has itself something of a dream quality, and the horrible reality of a nightmare. As the play draws to its end, and the net of defeat closes, another scene of revelry is promised, but in a nobler image; with a kind of metaphysical extravagance:

> . . . tonight I'll force
> The wine peep through their scars.[1]

It is an image that Donne would have understood.[2] Here in the galley Heroic Man is stripped down, even as Lear is stripped; Policy and Murder whisper for a moment in the background, and vanish; and two Captains prepare to desert their leader. Enobarbus will not *go ashore* with them, for the rat will not leave the ship yet. He flings his cap into the air:

> Hoo! says a'. There's my cap.
> *Menas.* Hoo! Noble captain, come.[3]
>   (Exeunt.

Is there a more ironical curtain in Shakespeare?

VII

So far, I suggest, we have these elements of a dream story: to the Puritan, a 'wretched business': to us, if we are honest with ourselves, a pattern which has some correspondence with our deep-rooted instincts. But, being this, the play would be no different from a score of other stories. My case is that its greatness rests on Shakespeare's technique of constantly putting forth tentacles from the dream into the reality. The contrast-values between the man of action set in a concentrated practical world, and the archetypal lover, are of a subtle and peculiar kind; and there is in fact a strongly rhythmical pattern which leads inexorably to the lyric utterance of the death-passages. What is uttered there is neither

---

[1] III.11.190.
[2] Compare, too, Yeats's ghost that may 'drink of the wine breath': 'All Souls' Night.'
[3] II.7.140.

THE IMAGES OF 'ANTONY AND CLEOPATRA'

rhetoric, nor stage pathos, nor a condonation of immorality; but something which does in fact constitute a transcending of this dream world, a projection beyond it into a world of ultimates where cardinal values move in a kind of elemental simplicity, but with constant and subtle counterpointing of the high and the low styles: which serve both to satirize the tragic dominant, and to restore it.

Let me elaborate this point a little. When we listen, at Hamlet's death, to the words

> Goodnight, sweet Prince,
> And flights of angels sing thee to thy rest!

we may well be in doubt whether that invocation has any meaning for a four-fold murderer, perhaps for a seducer too. Divinity, if indeed there be any in the bloodshot darkness of *Macbeth*, is submerged in a general ethic. Lear invokes vague heathen gods, who may or may not be just; yet he returns at the end to the virtue of patience. Othello prays to gods unspecified, and kneels to them, but we do not know them; nor does it appear that any of them has fixed 'a canon 'gainst self-slaughter'. Only in *Antony and Cleopatra* are the issues defined and free; liberated from the weedy tangled currents of Renaissance thought. It is a world of luck, the luck of the great and the not-so-great soldier, as all soldiers know:

> ... his quails ever
> Beat mine, inhoop'd, at odds.[1]

It is a world in which man's guardian spirit contends with other daimons, as Shakespeare, and Yeats, had learnt from Plutarch. As the net closes about the pair, we are aware of the gaiety of the Stoic tradition. We acknowledge a sublimation, untrammelled and uninhibited, of the death-wish which lies deep at the roots of our being, and whose sap rises when we are tired or old:

> Unarm, Eros; the long day's task is done,
> And we must sleep.[2]

[1] II.3.37.
[2] IV.12.35.

Its images are linked, as always, with love and with the bed: they crowd thickly about us:

> I will be
> A bridegroom in my death, and run into't
> As to a lover's bed.[1]

For whatever this sleep may be that comes when the armour is off, there is an emotional certainty of the lovers' reunion. Cleopatra, given the infinite room of the fifth act, refuses to relinquish this final power over her image and her destiny. 'Stay for me . . .' Cleopatra shows the gaiety of tragedy in its supreme form, tender, half-jesting:

> If she first meet the curléd Antony,
> He'll make demand of her, and spend that kiss
> Which is my heaven to have.[2]

for she has no illusions about her man. It is, I think, this strange kind of gaiety under the death-pressure, this mood which Yeats called 'the tragic reverie', which contributes so much to the balance of the play, a balance of energy and joy; yet all the while with its roots in reality. I must quote, and comment, to make my point.

VIII

You remember how Antony rallies his soldiers in defeat (the certain mark of a great commander) and how his qualities are rounded off by that act. Cleopatra does the same for her women, in a speech that I give in full to show these vibrating images of which we spoke before:

No more, but e'en a woman, and *commanded*	[The soldier's word: but also used of the emotions. But she will put on her robes and crown later. Now she is mourning. Is the drug and the aspic-breast image anticipated?]
By such poor passion as the maid that *milks*	
And does the meanest chares. It were for me	
To throw my sceptre at the injurious gods,	
To tell them that this world did equal theirs	

[1] IV.12.99.
[2] V.2.299.

THE IMAGES OF 'ANTONY AND CLEOPATRA'

Till they had stol'n our jewel. All's but naught;
Patience is sottish, and impatience does
Become a dog that's mad: then is it sin
To rush into the *secret house of death*,
Ere death dare come to us? How do you, women?
What, what! good cheer! Why, how now, Charmian!
My noble girls! Ah, women, women, look!
Our *lamp is spent*, it's out! Good sirs, take heart:
We'll bury him; and then, what's brave, what's noble,
Let's do it after the high Roman fashion,
And make death proud to take us.

[Think of Antony's 'The wrack dislimns . . .']

[Remember they are in the monument. Is there a memory of Juliet?]

[All length is *torture*, since the *torch* is out. And the lamp-oil-wick imagery is archetypal.]

The harlot-queen has shown us in the play this infinite variety of moods and moodiness. We have anger, jealousy, coquetry; railing, intrigue, cruelty; tenderness, cowardice, courage. She has shown the malicious unpredictability of a *gamin*, the regality of an empress. She draws her humanity from fear and weakness; and she must be able to transcend it by a supreme effort of the will; which yet shows always the oscillation, the advance and retreat, of the essentially human confronting the tragic fact.

IX

It would be possible to go on, indefinitely, in such considerations of the texture of these speeches; but for a last example, I ask you to consider this fragment of a scene in some little detail; noting the echoes from the part of the play which reverberates from the rocks deep under its surface:

Why, that's the way
To *fool* their preparation, and to conquer
Their most *absurd* intents.

[Ridicule, cutting both ways.]

THE LIVING IMAGE

Re-enter Charmian.

Now, Charmian,
Show me, my women, like a queen:
  go fetch
My best attires; I am again for Cydnus,
To meet Mark Antony. Sirrah Iras, go.
Now, noble Charmian, we'll dispatch
  indeed,
And when thou hast done this chare,
I'll *give thee leave*
To *play* till doomsday. Bring our
  crown and all.

[She is putting on her woman's *armour*. Is there a hint of the River-Death image, the classic resolution?]

[*Dispatch* – the word Antony has used at his suicide.]

[Charmian remembers this 'play' later.]

Exit Iras.   A Noise is heard.

Wherefore's this noise?

Enter one of the Guard

  Here is a rural fellow
That will not be denied your highness'
  presence:
He brings you figs.

Let him come in.   (*Exit Guard*)

  What poor an instrument
May do a noble deed! he brings me
  liberty.
My resolution's placed, and I have
  nothing
Of woman in me: now from head to
  foot
I am *marble-constant*; now the fleeting
  moon
No planet is of mine.

[Remember Charmian in the first scene.
'Excellent! I love long life better than figs!'. . . and the high-spirited bawdry of that early scene.]

[*Marble-constant* recalls statuary, perhaps the tomb; cold hard purity. The moon-imagery is everywhere. She has thrown over her temperamental qualities. But she has also overcome change, mutability. Consider 'The odds is gone,
And there is nothing left remarkable
Beneath the visiting moon.']

Then the Guard re-enters with the Clown. The protracted and inane conversation fulfills its normal dramatic function of getting on our

THE IMAGES OF 'ANTONY AND CLEOPATRA'

nerves. Throughout Cleopatra speaks in single sentences, sometimes in single words, with two curious half-frightened questions:

> Remember'st thou any that have died on't?
>
> Will it eat me?

She has, we are told, 'pursued conclusions infinite/of easy ways to die.' Perhaps all eastern potentates must do this. Then – *Re-enter Iras with a robe, crown, etc.*; and the sails fill as the full-freighted vessel turns to the open sea.

Give me my robe, put on my crown; I have	[The long varied tones of the 'o's]
Immortal longings in me; now no more	
The juice of Egypt's grape shall moist this lip:	['The wine of life is drawn, and the mere lees
Yare, yare, good Iras; quick. Methinks I hear	Is left this vault to brag of'.
Antony call; I see him rouse himself	The life-Egypt-wine cluster recurs continually.]
To praise my noble act; I hear him mock	
The luck of Caesar, which the gods give men	[Is this the final victory over Octavia?]
To excuse their after-wrath. Husband, I come:	
Now to that name my courage prove my title!	[The apotheosis]
I am fire and air; my other elements I give to baser life. So; have you done?	
Come then and take the last warmth of my lips.	
Farewell, kind Charmian; Iras, long farewell.	[The ritual kiss that takes and transmits life: Donne's 'last lamenting kiss'. Very few women could kiss a woman thus.]
(*Kisses them. Iras falls and dies*)	
Have I the aspic in my lips? Dost fall? If thou and nature can so gently part, The stroke of death is as a lover's *pinch*. Which hurts, and is desired. Dost thou lie still?	[She has used this image before: 'I that am with Phoebus' amorous *pinches* black

131

THE LIVING IMAGE

If thus thou vanishest, thou tell'st the world
It is not worth leave-taking.

Charmian. Dissolve, thick cloud, and rain; that I may say
The gods themselves do weep.

This proves me base:
If she first meet the *curlèd* Antony
He'll make demand of her, and spend that kiss
Which is my heaven to have. Come, mortal wretch,

(*To the asp, which she applies to her breast.*)

With thy sharp teeth this knot intrinsicate
Of life at once untie: poor venomous fool,
Be angry, and dispatch. O, couldst thou speak,
That I might hear thee call great Caesar ass
Unpolicied!

Charmian. O eastern star!

Cleopatra. Peace, peace!
Dost thou not see my baby at my breast,
That sucks the nurse asleep?

Charmian. O break! O, break!
As sweet as balm, as soft as air, as gentle –
O Antony! – Nay, I will take thee too.

Applying another asp to her arm)

And wrinkled deep in time.']

['Sometimes we see a cloud that's dragonish'
But is this not, also, the classic release – in tears and rain? Compare *The Ancient Mariner.*]
[*Curlèd* – new-barbered, ready for the feast: with its undertone of virility. 'that kiss'. *cf.* 'The nobleness of life is to do *this* . . . and 'Even this repays me'.
'*mortal*' – she picks up the clown's pun.]

[*cf.* Donne – 'This subtle knot, which makes us man.']
[*Fool* – a word one might apply to a child: as the Nurse in *Romeo and Juliet*.

A touch of human maliciousness: the gamin. And suddenly the mood changes.]

[Consider the layered meanings of the words to a Jacobean audience – though the Eastern Star is Venus.]
[The *ea*-sounds dimming down, 'No more, but e'en a woman . . .']

[Her heart? – and perhaps the dawn. The verse slows on the comma and the open modulating vowels, lingering on 'O Antony!']

THE IMAGES OF 'ANTONY AND CLEOPATRA'

What should I stay –

(*Dies*)

Charmian. In this vile world? So, fare thee well.

Now boast thee, death, in thy possession lies	[The image of personified Death, remembering Hamlet, and *Romeo and Juliet*.]
A lass unparallel'd. Downy windows, close;	['lass' – the milk-maid.]
And golden Phoebus never be beheld Of eyes again so royal! Your crown's awry I'll mend it, and then play.	[This is hysteria, spoken with a sob. But remember *Richard II* and the Holbein image of the Crown, from the Dance of Death. 'play' – 'I'll give thee leave To *play* till doomsday.']

There is, I believe, one hunting image at the end of the play, on which I comment with some hesitation. Caesar, for all his clinical efficiency, is prepared to pay tribute to Cleopatra dead:

> Bravest at the last,
> She levell'd at our purposes, and, being royal
> Took her own way.[1]

The commentators regard it, very properly, as being primarily an image from gunnery; she 'levelled' – aimed destructively – at the plans to capture her alive, for exhibition in a Roman triumph. But there is no reason whatever why images should not exist in superimposed layers which may lie, as it were, across the grain; there are countless instances in support.

The 'Great Hart' that had once been hunted by Royalty, and escaped, had the freedom of the forest for ever. No one would dare to chase it. Cleopatra has long been pursued by the baying hounds, as Julius Caesar was by the conspirators. Such a hart, embayed in a stream, against a cliff, or with its back to a large tree, sweeps the massive antlers, with a scythe-like motion, at the hounds. 'She levell'd at our purpose'. And being 'royal', mistress of two emperors, 'hunted' by them, she escaped into the Elysian Fields.

[1] v.2.332.

THE LIVING IMAGE

X

It has been said that only a poet can fully understand another poet. I know of two poets who have written well of the play. Masefield, taking the words that follow 'O eastern star', said of them that they were

> written at one golden time, in a gush of the spirit, when the man must have been trembling.

The other is Edith Sitwell, on the verse-texture of the passage; and I acknowledge my debt to her.

This scene that I have quoted seems to reveal so much. It throws back over nearly all the play, and draws it out to an incredible sharpness of focus on the transfiguration that both characters and issues undergo. Antony has passed to his Elysian Fields, and is now no more than a symbol, a gay triumphant masculine memory. He claimed our total sympathy at the instant of his double defeat; yielding to weariness, just as Macbeth does, in just such a meditative and complex speculation into the pattern of existence:

> Sometimes we see a cloud that's dragonish . . .

The scene of his death picks up and unifies by its ironic contrast that earlier scene. Let us remember it:

> *Antony.* Fulvia is dead.
> *Enobarbus.* Sir?
> *Antony.* Fulvia is dead.
> *Enobarbus.* Fulvia!
> *Antony.* Dead.
> *Enobarbus.* Why, sir, give the gods a thankful sacrifice.

And then this:

> *Mardian.* . . . she render'd life
> Thy name so buried in her.
> *Antony.* Dead, then?
> *Mardian.* Dead.
> *Antony.* Unarm, Eros; the long day's task is done,
> And we must sleep.

Throughout the play there is this tissue of echo-work, giving the sense

THE IMAGES OF 'ANTONY AND CLEOPATRA'

of depth and energy and ironic purpose; till irony and bitterness are swept away in a torrent of the essential humanity of the play. For I find in it, as in all the great tragedies, a circular or elliptical movement that begins and ends with elemental things. In Cleopatra's death scene all things meet: the Queen that puts on her splendid garment, a woman's armour, as she once buckled Antony for the fight. It is inevitable that she, the Queen, should bear the asp at her breast; should speak of it as she does with that image in which all humanity is comprehended; should surrender at last to motherhood and sleep and death. Underneath her speech there is a laughter which modulates itself most delicately and with flawless tact. She is aware that Antony's ghost is Antony still, and no more than a man; who will kiss Iras first if he is given the slightest chance. For it is a ghost's right to kiss a ghost, in those fields of flowers. Her impish quality is in the thought of Caesar baulked by death:

> That I might hear thee call great Caesar ass
> Unpolicied.

It changes to a smile at her own thought of the asp as her baby; the smile dying peacefully as the numbness of the poison suggests the exquisite sensuality of the nursing sleep. And as sleep grows heavy the thought of Antony and the meeting breaks across her thought: she rouses herself for a moment to apply the second asp. With Charmian's epitaph upon her all that went before is locked and sealed in hysteria: the 'lass' for the milkmaid, the simplicity of woman; the crown that's awry for the Queen. Then in a final stroke all the *opus Alexandrinum* of Renaissance decoration is picked up and made to serve Shakespeare's turn, the 'golden Phoebus' of a thousand drab sonnets. But here it is transformed. Gaiety has transfigured the dread of tragedy, and we are the richer for that knowledge.

XI

What, then, are we to say of this ending? It is unique in Shakespeare in that it is the tragedy of *The Woman's Part*. There are elements in it which make it different from the *lusis*, the Resolution, of any tragedy that I know.

The protagonists, man and woman are freed from the Christian fear of retribution, judgement: they are clear about one thing, that they will meet in the Elysian Fields. That meeting will be noble – 'Husband, I come!' and it will be gay, because it is lit with comedy; Caesar is fooled by Cleopatra's suicide. Cleopatra hastens because Antony ('curléd', as a lover should be for his bride)[1] might kiss Iras in the underworld if the maid precedes the mistress.

All the emotions – nobility, gaiety, the lamentations of those who surround them, are concentrated at a single point. Both have passed passed through the fires: rejection, defeat, vituperation. Both have lost the world. Both pass beyond that stage of renunciation of the world where values turn and re-set in a wholly new sphere. Through the poetry which they both speak as the death-pressure rises they each pass beyond the initial metaphysical questioning of reality, of the virtues of patience and suffering, into a world where their love is eternalized; where passion will never be staled; the cosmic imagery of the poetry comes, as it were, to rest. Does not the play tell us of what we all seek in dreams? – victory out of accomplished failure, ecstasy of desire perpetually fulfilled. It is well to quote Yeats, writing of another play:

> Shakespeare's persons . . . when the last darkness has gathered about them, speak out of an ecstasy that is one-half the self-surrender of sorrow, and one-half the last playing and mockery of the victorious sword before the defeated world.[2]

[1] See, *e.g. Canticles*, and Meredith's *Modern Love* (1862).
[2] *Essays and Introductions* (1961 p. 254).

Select Bibliography
Index

Select Bibliography

Arte of Angling Anon. 1577. Facsimile ed. G. E. Bentley. Princeton, 1958.
ARMSTRONG, E. A. *The Folklore of Birds*. London, 1958.
— *Shakespeare's Imagination*. London, 1946. Revised Edition, 1963.
ASCHAM, ROGER. *Toxophilus* (1545). Facsimile ed. E. G. Heath. Menston, Yorkshire, 1968.
BARRAT, R. *The Theory and Practice of Modern Wars* (1598).
BERT, E. *An Approved Treatise of Hawks and Hawking* (1619).
BLACKMORE, H. L. *British Military Firearms, 1650–1850*. London, 1961.
— *Firearms*. London, 1969.
— *Arms and Armour*. London, 1965.
BLUNDEVILLE, THOMAS. *The Four Chiefest Officers belonging to Horsemanship* (1577).
BLOME, R. *The Gentleman's Recreation* (1686).
— *Hawking or Faulconry* (1686). Facsimile. Preface by E. D. Cuming, London, 1929.
BOYNTON, LINDSAY. *The Elizabethan Militia, 1558–1638*. London, 1968.
CARMAN, W. Y. *A History of Firearms from the Earliest Times*. New York, 1955.
CIPOLLA, C. M. *Guns and Sails in the Early Phase of European Expansion, 1400–1700*. London, 1965.
COCKAYNE, T. *A Short Treatise of Hunting* (1591).
COOPER, SIR A. DUFF *Sergeant Shakespeare*. London, 1949.
COX, J. *The Royal Forests of England*. 1905.
CRUICKSHANK, C. G. *Elizabeth's Army*. Oxford, 1966.
ELYOT, SIR THOMAS. *The Book named The Gouernour* (1564).

GASTON DE FOIX (Gaston Phoebus). *Livre de Chasse*, translated as *The Master of Game* (1406–1413) by Edward, Second Duke of York, ed. Wm. A. and F. Baillie-Grohman, London, 1909.
GREENER, W. W. *The Gun and its Development*. London, 1881.
HALL, A. R. *Ballistics in the Seventeenth Century*. Cambridge, 1952.
HOLMES, MARTIN. *The Guns of Elsinore*. London, 1964.
HOTSON, J. LESLIE. *Shakespeare vs Shallow*. London, 1931.
JEFFERIES, RICHARD. *The Amateur Poacher*. London, 1879.
— *The Gamekeeper at Home*. London, 1881.
— *Bevis*. London, 1904.
JONES, H. A. and COPE, J. I. (ed.) *A History of the Royal Society* by Thomas Spratt. Missouri, 1958.
JORGENSEN, P. A. *Shakespeare's Military World*. Berkeley and C.U.P. 1956.
LATHAM, SIMON. *The Faulcon, or the Faulconer's Lure and Cure* (1615).
MACHIAVELLI. *The Arte of Warre* (transl. 1560).
MADDEN, D. H. *The Diary of Master William Silence*. London, 2nd ed. 1907.
MÂLE, EMILE. *The Gothic Image*. London, 1961.
MARKHAM, FRANCIS. *Five Decades of Epistles of War* (1622).
MARKHAM, GERVASE. *County Contentments* (1615).
— *The Pleasures of Princes, or Good Men's Recreations* (1614).
MARKLAND, ABRAHAM. *Pteryphlegia, or the Art of Shooting Flying* (1727).
MASCALL, LEONARD. *Booke of Fishing with a Hooke and Line* (1590).
MATTINGLY, GARRETT. *The Defeat of the Spanish Armada*. London, 1959.
OMAN, SIR CHARLES. *A History of the Art of War in the Sixteenth Century*. London, 1937.
OMMUNDSEN H. and ROBINSON E. H. *Rifles and Ammunition*. London, 1915.
ONIONS, C. T. (ed.) *Shakespeare's England*. 2 vols. Oxford, 1916.
PARTRIDGE, ERIC. *Shakespeare's Bawdy*. London, 1955.
PAYNE-GALLWEY, SIR R. *The Crossbow*. London, 1903.
PETERSON, H. L. *The Book of the Gun*. London, 1966.
RICHE, BARNABE. *A Pathway for Military Practice* (1587). Facsimile, Amsterdam, 1969.

SELECT BIBLIOGRAPHY

SITWELL, DAME EDITH. *A Notebook on W. Shakespeare*. London, 1948.
SITWELL, SACHEVERELL. *The Hunters and the Hunted*. London, 1947.
STONE, LILY B. *English Sports and Recreations*. Washington, 1960. Folger Library Booklet.
TILANDER, GUNNAR. *Julians Barnes Boke of Hunting*. Cynegetica XI, Karlshamn, 1967.
TURBERVILLE, GEORGE. *The Booke of Faulconrie or Hawking* (1575).
— *The Noble Arte of Venerie or Hunting* (1611).
WARNER, P. A. W. *Sieges of the Middle Ages*. London, 1968.
*WEBB, HENRY J. *Elizabethan Military Science*. Wisconsin, 1965.
WHITE, T. H. *The Goshawk*, London, 1951.
WHITEHORN, PETER. *Certain Waies for the orderyng of Soldiers in battelray* (1562).
WILSON, EDMUND. *The Wound and the Bow*. London, 1952.

*An admirable bibliography of military writing of the period is given here.

Index

Agincourt, 75, 77, 81–2, 84, 89, 113
Amos, Book of, 59
Anderson, R. L., 18
Aristotle, 84
Armstrong, E. A.
— *Folklore of Birds*, ix, 12, 41
— *Shakespeare's Imagination*, ix, 25n, 32, 33, 54, 62n
Arte of Angling, The (1577), 56, 57, 58, 61
Ascham, ix, 1, 77, 80, 81, 85

Bacon, *Friar*, 96
ballads, 2, 3, 16, 21, 72
Barbary Horse, 71, 72n, 76
Bellini, 27, 33n
Berners, Juliana, 7, 9, 56
Bible, 3, 23, 25n, 35, 65, 70n, 122
birdlime, 12
Blackwood's Magazine, x, 84n
Blake, William, 8, 66
Blome, R., ix, 7, 19n, 22, 28, 31, 37, 38, 39, 45
Boke of St. Albans, The, ix, 7, 9, 27n, 31n, 48, 56, 61, 78n
Book of Fires, The, 96

Browne, *Sir* T., 87
Boynton, Lindsay, ix, 103n
Burton, Robert, 68

Caesar, Julius, 115
Campbell, Roy, 3, 15
cannon, 98–100
Canticles, Book of, 17n, 62, 136n
Castiglione, 55
chain shot, 98
Charlecote, 56, 62
Chaucer, 10, 19
Clark, 32
Coleridge, 6, 132
Collier, 118
Columbus, 14n
company (*org.*), 111
Compleat Angler, The, 59
Conyers, D., 55n
Cooper, *Sir* H. Duff, 88
I Corinthians, 112
II Corinthians, 59n
Cotswold Games, 48–50
coursing, 13
Coverley, *Sir* R. de, 44n
Creçy, 77, 82, 89

INDEX

Croce, 87
crossbow, 78
Cruickshank, C. G., 96n, 113
Cuming, H. D., 19, 22

Da Vinci, Leonardo, 103
Denny, William, 50
Digges, Leonard, 104, 106, 115
Donne, 26, 59, 92, 98n, 101n, 132
Dryden, 120
Du Bartas, 67
Dürer, 64, 123
Duthie, 27n
Dyce, 47

Elizabethan Sonnets, 90
Ellacombe, H. N., 55
enseamed, 38
Ephesians, Ep. to, 116n
Exodus, Book of, 52n

Foix, Gaston de, ix, 7, 8, 41, 44, 45
Forester, C. S., 98n
Forsyth, *Rev. A.*, 18
Freud, 65
Fuseli, 65

Garrard, W., 89, 104, 115
Golden Bough, The, 86
Gosson, 117
Graves, Robert, 65

Hardy, Thomas, 72, 80
Harfleur, 84, 100
Henryson, 17

Herèdia, de, 121
Hogarth, 12n
Holbein, 133
Holmes, Martin, x
Homer, 3, 90
Honorius of Autun, 60
Hopkins, Gerard Manley, 21, 24
Hotson, Leslie, 56n
Housman, A. E., 65, 80
Hughes, Ted, 24
Humphreys, A. R., 34n, 35

Ibsen, 5, 66
imp (*vb*), 32, 36

Jefferies, Richard, 5, 88
Jeremiah, Book of, 70
Job, Book of, 59–60, 64
Johnson, Samuel, x, 49, 104, 118
Jonson, Ben, 14
Jorgenson, P., ix, 88, 109, 110, 116n
Jorrocks, 13

Judges, Book of, 51n

King, *Bishop*, 112
Kings, Book of, 81
Kipling, Rudyard, 16, 88, 98n

Leviticus, Book of, 9
'Longinus', 35n, 59
Lovat Scouts, 8

Macedon, Philip of, 115
Machiavelli, 97, 115

INDEX

Madden, D. H., ix, 1, 3, 14n, 21n, 32, 47, 50n, 55n, 68, 69, 72n
Mâle, Emile, 60
Masefield, John, 134
Mascall, L., 56
Master of Game, The, ix, 7, 41
Markham, Gervase, ix, 7, 50, 69, 93, 95, 100, 104, 106, 108, 111, 116
Markland, Francis, 19
Matthew, Saint, 60
Mead, H. C. H., x
Meredith, George, 136
Milton, 6
Morris, William, 82, 90
Muir, K., 65, 71

Nashe, Thomas, 4, 13, 58n
Nieuport, 98

Odysseus, 86
Ovid, 14, 26

Park, Trevor, x
Partridge, Eric, 62
Payne-Galway, *Sir* R., 79n
Peterson, H. L., 103
Plato, 6, 117
Plutarch, 118, 119, 127
Porphyry, 38
powder, 95–6
Proverbs, Book of, 32
Psalms, Book of, 86
Pterephlegia, 19

Rabelais, 68
rations, 114

Revelation, Book of, 66
Rhymer, 118
Robin Hood, 85n
Roy, J., 32
Rubens, 119
Rylands, G. H. W., 45

2 Samuel, Book of, 35, 114n
Simenon, Georges, 11n
Sitwell, Edith, 134
Sitwell, Sacheverell, 52
Shakespeare's England, 47
Shakespeare
 POEMS
  Sonnets, 99n
  Venus and Adonis, 19, 50n, 51, 67, 68, 76
 PLAYS
  Antony and Cleopatra, ix, 29, 30n, 38, 45, 58, 69, 73–4, 115, 117ff.
  All's Well That Ends Well, 72, 90
  As You Like It, 19, 71
  Comedy of Errors, 47, 70
  Coriolanus, 48, 53, 106, 107, 113, 116
  Cymbeline, 49n, 90n
  Hamlet, 2, 3, 11, 12, 26, 28, 32, 37, 38, 47, 50, 53, 73, 85, 93, 99, 100n, 105, 133
  I Henry IV, 34, 48, 73, 75, 77, 87, 98, 102, 104, 109
  II Henry IV, 47, 65, 69, 70, 80, 94, 115
  Henry V, 48, 70, 74, 75, 88, 100, 103, 108, 109, 113, 114, 115
  I Henry VI, 113
  II Henry VI, 22, 23, 31
  Henry VIII, 11, 97, 99
  Julius Caesar, 9, 23, 124

INDEX

Shakespeare—continued
  King John, 17, 96, 104
  King Lear, 5, 45, 51, 65, 79, 80, 81, 113
  Love's Labour's Lost, 15, 31n, 38, 74–5, 78
  Macbeth, 25, 28, 29, 53, 65, 66, 67, 71, 111, 121
  Measure for Measure, 31, 32, 36, 59, 61, 73
  Merchant of Venice, 75
  The Merry Wives of Windsor, 51
  Midsummer Night's Dream, 19, 33, 41, 42, 74, 83, 87
  Much Ado, 13, 19, 39, 40, 43–4, 59, 74
  Othello, 17, 18, 23, 25, 34, 45, 100, 101, 102, 107, 108, 115, 125
  Pericles, 38, 99
  Richard II, 9, 36, 71, 72, 75, 114n, 133
  Richard III, 10
  Romeo and Juliet, 10, 26, 27, 49, 70, 83, 91, 132
  Taming of the Shrew, 25, 46, 68
  Tempest, 11, 37, 44, 46, 58, 114n, 121n
  Timon of Athens, 50
  Titus Andronicus, 54
  Troilus and Cressida, 7, 38, 115
  Twelfth Night, 2, 4, 17n, 46, 47, 51, 52, 61, 78, 83n, 120
  Two Gentlemen of Verona, 46
  Winter's Tale, 37, 38, 52, 62, 74, 99
Samuel, Book of, 114
Shaw, G. B., 117
'Shot-on-Horseback', 102–3
Somerville and Ross, 55
Sophocles, 2
Sprat, 96
springes, 10
Spencer, T. J. B., ix
Spenser, Edmund, 1, 62, 112
Steevens, 32
Stevenson, R. L., 57n
'Stone-bow', 79
Stubbes, 117
Stubbs, George, 67
Swinburne, 16
Synge, J. M., 3, 80

'Tartar's Bow', 83
Taylor, Jeremy, 23
Thomas, Dylan, 33, 61
Thomas, Edward, 5
Tilander, Gunnar, 7n
Titian, 119
Turberville, ix, 7, 51

Velasquez, 90n
'Voluntaries', 105–6

Wagner, 66
Wallace, W. A., 32
Walton, Isaak, 7, 59
Warner, P. A. W., 82
Webb, H. J., ix, 77, 81, 88, 89, 96, 98, 104, 106n, 115n
Webster, 92
Wellington, Duke of, 39
West Point, ix, x
'Weston Martyr', 84, 85, 108
wheel-lock, 103
White, T. H., x, 20, 24, 25, 30, 36n, 40

INDEX

Whitehorne, Peter, 96, 97, 99
'Wild Hunt, The', 41, 66
Williams, Sir R., 81, 101
Wilson, Edmund, 86
Wilson, J. Dover, 27n, 48
Winny, J., 31n, 32n
Wodehouse, P. G., 14
Wordsworth, 2, 3
Wright, Aldis, 32

Xenophon, 115

Yeats, W. B., 1, 4, 5, 24, 33, 54, 66, 70, 86n, 117, 126n, 127, 128, 136

Zechariah, Book of, 66

For Product Safety Concerns and Information please contact our EU representative GPSR@taylorandfrancis.com
Taylor & Francis Verlag GmbH, Kaufingerstraße 24, 80331 München, Germany

www.ingramcontent.com/pod-product-compliance
Lightning Source LLC
Chambersburg PA
CBHW051647230426
43669CB00013B/2471